W9-AQL-930

FRONT RANK

Written for

THE NORTH CAROLINA CONFEDERATE CENTENNIAL COMMISSION by

GLENN TUCKER

With illustrations by Bill Ballard

THE NORTH CAROLINA CONFEDERATE CENTENNIAL COMMISSION • RALEIGH

Library of Congress Catalog Card Number 62-22313

Manufactured in the United States of America
Heritage Printers, Inc.
Charlotte, N. C.

Contents

"In the number of soldiers furnished, in the discipline, courage and loyalty and difficult service of those soldiers, in amount of material and supplies contributed, in the good faith and moral support of her people at large, and in all the qualities which mark self sacrifice, patriotism and devotion to duty, North Carolina is entitled to stand where her troops stood in battle, behind no State, but in the front rank of the Confederation, aligned and abreast with the best, the foremost and the bravest."

—Governor Zebulon Vance

THE FAITH OF A STATE IN A CAUSE

Zebulon B. Vance, the rugged, dynamic, stormy war Governor of North Carolina and one of the dominant civilian figures of the Confederacy, told the story of Thomas Calton of Burke County, relating it among his many postwar recollections at the gathering place of the old Southern soldiers at White Sulphur Springs, West Virginia.

Calton's sons entered the Confederate service one by one, and one by one they fell to Northern bullets. At length the fifth son, Benjamin, youngest and fairest, "bright-haired, blue eyed," the remaining treasure of the old man's heart, put on the gray uniform and went away.

When the news arrived that he, too, had been killed in battle, all in the community dreaded to carry such a story of desolation to the enfeebled father. A close friend and neighbor finally was prevailed upon to deliver the heavy message.

But Thomas Calton of Burke was the type of man who, in Vance's words, "ennobles our humanity." The winds of misfortune might bend him but he would not break. Undismayed that his male issue had been extinguished in the sacred name of freedom, he uttered only a single note of despair, then called to his delicate, sickly son-in-law, whom the army already had rejected. Trembling with emotion, he issued his command sternly:

"Get your knapsack, William. The ranks must be filled!"

Vance used the incident to portray the old man's fidelity. But by it he illustrated much more than the steadfastness of an individual or family. It was a story characteristic of a State through four years of one of the most desperately fought wars of human history; a war which North Carolina did not foment or seek, which she entered late in the secession movement more from a sense of loyalty and devotion to her sister Southern commonwealths than from anger against the Federal Union; but which she pursued with a burning fervor and unabating energy until the final bugle blew the sad notes of recall at Appomattox — until tens of thousands of her young men filled nameless graves, her wealth was dissipated, her industry wrecked, her agriculture devastated, her entire economy laid prostrate, and most of her surviving citizens rendered altogether destitute.

Such a war many have wanted forgotten. It was followed by the unhappy Reconstruction years which resulted more from the excesses of an immoderate Congress than from the vengeance of a victorious Northern people, during which the South was administered in what has been termed, after the provincial rule of Oriental despots, "military satrapies." The postwar years gave cause for resentment in many hearts deeper than any which abided from defeat on the field of battle.

Such sectional rancor led even in Vance's day to an outcry that the war and its depressing aftermath should be buried deep in the public consciousness and obliterated from functions and ceremonies, so that all memory of it would eventually pass away. Some seemed to discern that even in the honors being paid the war dead there was a purpose "to keep alive the fires of sectional bitterness, and feed a spirit of ill-faith toward our present duties."

But the dauntless leader who had been the wartime governor challenged this attitude and called to the attention of the people the duty they owed their posterity to record and nourish and freshen the truth about the State's heroic efforts:

"The light which our conflict will afford them in grappling with many difficulties of the future, will be a lamp to their feet. . . . Surely there is in our story food to satisfy the reflective and to fire the hearts of the brave, for many generations."

Though this relentless, internecine struggle pitted neighbor against neighbor, brother against brother, father against son; though it involved carnage and brutality and episodes which the fair-minded would like expunged from the record; there was about it a vast treasure of triumph, tragedy, noble example, humor, pathos, sacrifice and at times saintliness that should be remembered and preserved as splendid and vital parts of the American tradition.

The unyielding resolution, faithfulness to duty and dedication to cause which characterized the young soldiers sent far afield from

North Carolina homes — from mountain cabins and white columned plantation mansions alike, most of them youths who had no part in the agitation and discord and many who knew little of what brought on the conflict — is a heritage that will inspire Americans as long as the Nation and the State endure. None can marvel at what they sacrificed without experiencing a solemn period of honest thoughtfulness and something of a personal and spiritual rededication.

North Carolina's main part in this agonizing ordeal of combat was in heeding the admonition of citizen Thomas Calton and "keeping the ranks filled." Though only third in population among the seceding states and possessing only one-ninth of the total population of the Confederacy, North Carolina supplied one-sixth of the soldiers and sustained the heaviest loss in casualties among the Southern states. Having a white population of 629,942 in 1860 — the Negro population being ineligible for army service — and 115,000 voters, the State sent 133,905 soldiers, by the old roster count, into the ranks. The rosters are being rechecked and the number may in fact aggregate about 185,000, as many omissions have been discovered. "More volun-

teers than voters" could be the cry of several states, but emphatically of North Carolina.

Her contributions along many lines were immense — in supplying manpower; in producing food and provisioning the armies, especially General Lee's forces in Virginia; in manufacturing textiles and other critical materials; in maintaining at Wilmington virtually an open port for blockade-running and thereby providing a lifeline for medicines and a host of essential items for which the South had been long dependent on foreign countries and the North; in offering up her financial resources in taxes and bonds; and, not least among many others, in the inspirational leadership and dogged determination of Zebulon Vance and his North Carolina associates, who, while often declared to be a thorn in the side of the Richmond government, were always intent on victory and were, in fact, one of the main obstacles to the triumphant march of the large Northern armies. They had burning faith in their cause.

This inspirational quality should not be underestimated. It was one of the warm human elements in a newly organized country whose government was often disposed to be aloof from the ordinary run of people. It seems not unlikely that Vance, with his dynamic personality, remarkable stumping ability, intense patriotic ardor, and the affectionate hold he had on the people of his own State, could have succeeded Jefferson Davis as President of the Confederacy had the cause triumphed and had he so desired. Lee had already eliminated himself positively from politics and Jefferson Davis was restricted by the constitution to a single term.

Who else but Vance? His eloquence could be judged by the tour he made visiting different regiments of the Army of Northern Virginia. None could possibly have aroused greater fervor. Lee had Jeb Stuart accompany him and Stuart declared that, judged by responsiveness of soldiers, "Vance is the greatest orator that ever lived." Lee himself must have caught the inspiration that swept through the army, for he was quoted as saying that Vance's visit was worth a reinforcement of 50,000 recruits.

But the State's main contribution was in military effort, and it was not seen primarily within her own borders, though there was sporadic fighting along the coast and later in the interior. On the outer rim of the Confederacy, in the front rank of the firing line, North Carolina made her stand.

ANSWERING THE CALL TO ARMS

NORTH CAROLINA SECEDED May 20, 1861, after moving by slow stages to that determination. Whether or not the action was constitutional and justified will never be answered. All the voluminous writing on this subject both before and after the conflict has been inconclusive. The right of self-determination even now is held to be inherent; yet all share gladly in the glories of a strong, united Nation.

The situation may have been aptly summed up by one of the greatest of North Carolina governors, Charles B. Aycock, when he said: "There are two subjects on which I take it there can be no debate — that the States had a right to secede in 1861, and that they no longer have that right."

In 1861 the decision, as far as North Carolina was concerned, was abrupt and virtually inescapable. While the gathering forces of secession had been shaping themselves over a long period in all parts of the South, they were countered in North Carolina by widespread, stanch adherence to the Union. The momentous question had to be determined suddenly, after the firing on Fort Sumter, when President Lincoln called on the State for two regiments to help subdue her sister Southern states.

Great as was Lincoln's statesmanship, undoubtedly it was questionable judgment and procedure in that hour of high emotions and critical decisions to assess North Carolina with a quota of men to fight her neighbors on all sides. The action silenced the strong Union elements which to that hour had been dominating public opinion in favor of preserving the Union. Sharp indeed was the veering of public sentiment. The abrupt change after Lincoln's call was evidenced by the words of Vance, then a second term congressman representing the mountain district and an ardent campaigner for adherence to the old government. Civil strife he held to be folly. But while he was speaking against secession, with his hand upraised in a pleading gesture for the Union, someone handed him the news of Lincoln's call for 75,000 troops. Like the rest of the State, he stiffened, then resisted. The hour of moderation suddenly passed. Revolt took the place of compliance.

"When my hand came down from that gesticulation," he said, "it fell slowly and sadly by the side of a secessionist." If war had to come, he, like Lee, preferred to be with his own people. He described the transformation which swept across the Southern states: "The argument having ceased and the sword being drawn, all classes in the South united as by magic, as only a common danger could unite them."

And so North Carolina, which in the 1860 election had maintained a strong Union stand, and only as recently as February 28, 1861, had decided by popular vote against secession by electing a preponderance of unionists to a proposed convention, now, only two and a half months later, almost with unanimity except in some of the western counties, cut its ties with the old government and went its own way.

Major James G. Martin

Governor John W. Ellis emphatically declined to supply Lincoln with the troops. Everywhere steadfast old unionists became fervent new secessionists. All of the State's thirteen newspapers espoused the secession cause.

Whatever the antipathies of many citizens may have been against the Washington government over slavery or other issues in the past, these were not of much consequence in the turn of events in April and May, 1861. The overt measure which took North Carolina out of the Union was not slavery, nor the tariff, nor John Brown's raid, nor the formation of the Montgomery government, nor the firing on Fort Sumter, but President Lincoln's call for volunteers, coupled with his decree blockading the Southern ports.

Once the matter was decided there was wild jollification. Guns boomed, bells rang and parades moved through the streets. It was plowing time but plows stood idle in the fields. Lads came down from the hills with old flintlocks. The State legislature on May 1, 1861 — ahead of consummating the secession — provided for raising ten regiments to serve for the duration of the war, then summoned 50,000 additional volunteers for one year's service.

Men began digging trenches to defend the coastal cities. Major James G. Martin, one arm gone from his gallant service at Churubusco in the Mexican War, was soon appointed Adjutant General of

AMERICAN TELEGRAPH COMPANY.

TERMS AND CONDITIONS ON WHICH MESSAGES ARE RECEIVED BY THIS COMPANY FOR TRANSMISSION.

The public are notified that, in order to guard against mistakes in the transmission of messages, every message of importance ought to be repeated by being sent back from the station at which it is to be received to the station from which it is originally sent. Half the usual price for transmission will be charged for repeating the message, and while this Company, will as heretofore, use every precaution to ensure correctness, it will not be responsible for mistakes or delays in the transmission or delivery of repeated messages beyond five hundred times the amount paid for sending the message, nor will it be responsible for mistakes or delays in the transmission of unrepeated messages, from whatever cause they may arise, nor for the delays arising from interruptions in the workings of its telegraphs, nor for any mistakes or omission of any other Company over whose lines a message is to be sent to reach the place of destination. All messages will hereafter be received by this Company for transmission subject to the above conditions.

J. KENDALL, Gen'l Sup't,
145 BROADWAY, N. Y.

E. S. SANFORD, Pres't,
145 BROADWAY, N. Y.

Received at Raleigh April 15th 1861 at o'clock minutes.
By telegraph from Washington To J. W. Ellis

War Department April (15th)
Call made on you by tonights mail for two (2) Regiments of Military for immediate service.

Simon Cameron
Secty of War

Courtesy Southern Historical Collection

North Carolina troops and no designation could have been happier. A native of Elizabeth City, Martin was graduated from West Point in 1840 and remained in the Regular Army until his State seceded. His energy, along with that of Zeb Vance, was in large measure responsible for the extraordinary record of North Carolina in supplying and equipping men for the Confederate armies. Known as "Old One Wing," he eventually found field duty in western North Carolina and fought the last battle in the State at Waynesville.

Throughout the spring of 1861 the towns were in a frenzy of organizing and preparing. While the cheers rang for secession, the State assumed its warlike posture. With fife and bugle, drum roll and silken banner, companies marched and regiments assembled. Camps were established hurriedly and the military units, some ancient with traditions dating back to the Revolution, others green as mountain meadows in both officers and men, gradually began the movement toward Raleigh and the promised fighting front in Virginia.

When excitement had been promised earlier around Charleston and the ominous threat of war had first filled the air, Commandant

Daniel Harvey Hill of the North Carolina Military Institute at Charlotte, an enterprising educator and soldier who had come to the Old North State originally from South Carolina, determined to make a personal reconnaissance. He went to Charleston, talked with Beauregard, and returned loaded with information, for which the entire cadet corps assembled, some of them already clamoring for combat. He restrained them: "Young gentlemen, if there be one hostile gun fired at Sumter, you will see enough of it before the war is over."

Now the gun had sounded at Sumter. Never was a summons answered with more alacrity than by the North State youth. The ranks of the first ten regiments were quickly filled. The recruiting continued until, in all, North Carolina put eighty-four regiments into the field. They served on far-flung battlefields, and most honorably and effectively at Antietam and Gettysburg, which must be accounted the two great battles of North Carolina history. How notable were their contributions on those fields may be seen from the fact that one-fourth of Lee's losses at Gettysburg, the most costly battle of the war, were of North Carolina troops.

But there was little thought of death in May and June of 1861, when companies drilled, batteries of polished cannon fired trial salvos, cavalrymen brought up their favorite mounts and formed squadrons, and spirits burned with intense patriotic ardor equal to a religious zeal.

Chapter

A LIFE GOES ON THE ALTAR

THUS WITH CHEERS, exciting festivities, and buoyant confidence the soldiers marched away. In the fighting there were high points. The first came at Bethel. There near Virginia tidewater, the First North Carolina Volunteers gave to the Confederacy the initial sacrifice on a field of glory.

The First North Carolina had been brought together from different counties and mustered in at Raleigh. The Charlotte *Democrat* commented: "This regiment is said to be the finest looking body of men ever assembled in the State." No doubt the hearsay was accurate. When three of the companies, en route from Raleigh to Richmond, passed through Petersburg, the *Express* of that city noticed that each had its full complement of 109 men, and added: "If we may form an opinion of the whole regiment by the material and appearance of the . . . three companies, we would unhesitatingly pronounce it to be one of the finest in the world."

These companies were the Lafayette Light Infantry of Fayetteville, the Fayetteville Independent Infantry, and the Southern Stars. The last was from Lincolnton and the most lustrous of its stars was its second lieutenant, soon risen to captain, Robert F. Hoke, destined to be one of the greatest soldiers North Carolina ever produced. When the remainder of the regiment went through Petersburg a few days later, the newspaper confirmed its earlier judgment.

The regiment was reassembled in Richmond, then moved down the Peninsula to Yorktown where it displayed itself on the plain. One of the reporters found that editors, lawyers, and doctors were in the ranks as privates. The distinguished Carolina minister, the Reverend Edwin A. Yates, served as chaplain.

Other companies were the Edgecombe Guards, the Hornet's Nest Rifles of Charlotte, the Charlotte Grays, Orange Light Infantry, Buncombe Riflemen (western North Carolina had joined in prayers when it left the Asheville public square), the Burke Rifles, and the Enfield Blues. Colonel Daniel Harvey Hill, pious, bellicose and capable, West Point classmate of Longstreet, Rosecrans, Doubleday, Lafayette McLaws, Alexander P. Stewart, and others of high distinction in both armies and professor of mathematics at Davidson College before becoming commandant of the military school at Charlotte, was in command. He had married a daughter of Robert Hall Morrison, the first president of Davidson College. Thomas J. Jackson had taken as his second wife another of Morrison's daughters. The two generals and brothers-in-law were compatible and were often thrown together in the army.

Another West Point graduate, Charles C. Lee of the class of 1856, South Carolina born, was lieutenant colonel. He would fall a year later at Glendale, Virginia. A Virginian, James H. Lane, stellar graduate in the class of 1854 at Virginia Military Institute, who had gone to Charlotte to teach under Hill, was major and drill-master.

The regiment reached Richmond before North Carolina seceded and fought its first battle three days after the State merged its forces with the Confederacy. On its arrival it was technically only an ally to the Virginians under Robert E. Lee and not a part of the Confederate forces under Beauregard.

The battle on June 10 at Bethel (called the battle of Big Bethel in the North) was an exciting clash at the time, but few would have lifted an eyelash over it a little later in the war. Brigadier General John Bankhead Magruder commanded the Confederates on the lower Peninsula, but Colonel D. H. Hill conducted the engagement. When Hill took the First North Carolina to Yorktown, Magruder ordered it forward with a Virginia battery of five guns and some other small detachments, the force aggregating about 1,400 officers and men, to Big Bethel Church just behind a branch of the Back River. The church was about midway between the York and James rivers, situated on one of the roads from Yorktown to Newport News. Big Bethel was thirteen miles from Yorktown and about eight from Hampton and equidistant from Newport News. The five guns Magruder sent along with Hill were commanded by Major George W. Randolph, Thomas Jefferson's grandson who, Hill in his enthusiasm

Henry Lawson Wyatt,
"First at Bethel . . ."

after the engagement said, had "no superior as an artillerist in any country." This was the period of lavishness and felicitations, before the earnestness of deadly war brought the restraint of realism to battle reports.

The Federals were at Newport News and Hampton under Major General Benjamin F. Butler. Butler had not yet become distasteful to the South because of his frictions with the civilian population of New Orleans. He was a Massachusetts politician and congressman who had been pushed ahead to solidify in the North the Democratic party's adherence to the war. At Big Bethel (there was a Little Bethel also, a Negro church five miles down the road toward Newport News) Hill learned that Butler was moving toward him, intent, as some have had it, on marching up the Peninsula and right into Richmond. By coincidence, Big Bethel was the name of the church where Hill had been baptized, and easily remembered. Hill threw up some slight works behind the creek in front of the church, sent out patrols, and waited.

Butler had a reconnaissance made of the position, then dispatched Brigadier General Ebenezer W. Peirce with converging regiments, one the celebrated Seventh New York, to oust the Confederates from their advanced post at Little Bethel and their main camp at Big Bethel. Major Lane meantime had been scouting ahead for Hill with a part of the First Regiment which passed within sight of Hampton, then on the return to Bethel had a brush with the Northern force. It was bloodless for Lane, but the Federals left behind three dead when they retired. The first Northern prisoner, "a stout, ugly fellow from Troy, N. Y.," was brought in and was alleged to aver that he "had nothing against the South, but somebody had to be soldiers."

Peirce's men became confused in their advance, and two of the Federal regiments fired on each other. Finally they reached and carried Little Bethel, which already had been vacated by the Southern skirmishers, and then came up against Hill's defenses. There they fought something of a battle and retired. Randolph's guns did good work and Hill's infantry maintained a strong musketry fire. A good deal of bravery was displayed by green troops on both sides.

Butler conceded that things were mismanaged by the Northerners, who had, by his account, six times as many as their adversaries. But after the Federal artillery commander, Lieutenant John T. Greble of the Regular Army, had been killed there did not appear to be, according to Butler's complaint, "a head more than a cabbage head

to undertake to do anything." His idea was that if his force had possessed enterprise it could have marched right through Hill's position. After a few abortive advances the Federal officers conferred and decided the troops were tired from marching and also were hungry, and therefore Peirce ordered the retirement. Heavily outnumbered, the Confederates were unable to pursue. The Federals undertook no further offensive. Such was Bethel.

The Federals lost eighteen killed, fifty-three wounded, and five missing, three of whom were prisoners the Confederates captured. The loss included a gallant Federal staff officer, Major Theodore Winthrop, who with two soldiers accompanying him, assailed the Confederate earthworks with his drawn sword, trying to inspire a turning force sent against Hill's left. The two privates went down with their leader. Winthrop was supposed to have been shot by a North Carolina drummer boy with a borrowed gun.

The Confederates lost one killed and nine wounded. This single battle death in Hill's regiment occurred when a detail went forward to burn a house that was providing shelter for enemy sharpshooters in front of the line. Hill had Captain John L. Bridgers of Company A, the Edgecombe Guards, call for volunteers. Five men, with Corporal George T. Williams at their head, rushed forward with hatchet and matches. A volley greeted them from their left, and Henry L. Wyatt of Tarboro was dropped, mortally wounded. He died without recovering consciousness, the first Confederate soldier killed in battle in the long and dreary war.

Others had fallen a few days earlier in skirmishes which were scarcely rated as engagements, but word about such casualties did not seem to spread across the South. Mainly they were later discoveries from the statistics.

Wyatt was heralded as the first. All knew he would not be the last. But who could look down the vista of crude crosses and hastily mounded graves — 41,000 for dead from North Carolina alone — and picture the grisly sacrifice that would be made by both sides, Americans against Americans, fighting for what they believed to be right, and what they understood to be the cause of freedom? As the war continued and the casualty lists mounted, this twenty-year-old youth became a symbol. Camps were named in his honor. His picture hangs in the Hall of History in Raleigh today, and there is a monument to him on Capitol Square. More than that, his sacrifice, plus the firm stand of D. H. Hill's regiment, gave to North Carolina the first phrase of its worthy motto, "First at Bethel, Farthest at Gettysburg . . . Last at Appomattox."

The aftermath of Bethel was greater than the battle. The Richmond *Dispatch* saw it as "one of the most extraordinary victories in the annals of war." Hill was promoted to brigadier general. The Virginia legislature eulogized the North Carolina regiment. The *Richmond Whig* found the Southerners "cool and determined as Bonaparte's veterans." A wave of exultation swept across the South, attended by lavish laudation of the North Carolina soldiers. In the North, critics inveighed against Lincoln's generals. But the greater, more deadly battle of Manassas was less than six weeks ahead, and soon Bethel was forgotten amid the immense orgies of bloodletting of the next four years. Still, it did check the Federal movement up the Peninsula until McClellan transported his great army there in the spring of the following year.

THE SIXTH PERFORMS AT MANASSAS

After Bethel came Manassas, battle of heartbreaks. There was heartbreak for the Union because of the staggering defeat suffered in what it believed would be an easy victory; heartbreak for the Confederacy because the invitation to follow up the triumph was wantonly neglected.

Battle of heartbreaks because the first long casualty lists went across the states, carrying poignant grief and the startling intelligence that the conflict would not be brief, local and moderate, as the optimists hoped, but merciless and sanguinary, as the realists had predicted. In the words of Vance, a little later it would be "War! War!! War!!!"

Generals and colonels were shot down. The first of the great funeral processions — that of Francis Bartow, beloved former mayor of Savannah, who had helped organize the Confederate army as chairman of the House Military Affairs Committee of the Montgomery Congress — moved down the Richmond streets. His widow fainted when his charger was led past with empty saddle. Soon thousands of saddles would be emptied in this stern war. The body of Barnard E. Bee was taken back to South Carolina for burial, a sacrifice always to be remembered because he had called a man "Stonewall."

Battle of sorrows, battle of shattered hopes, of jubilation and despair, pageantry and buffoonery! Manassas, or Bull Run, is in retrospect the *opéra bouffe* episode of American history. Still, there was an abundance of stanch courage and supreme sacrifice by men who had never experienced war. Bee's brigade played a key role, and in it the Sixth North Carolina was so conspicuous that it might be said the fortunes of the battle turned on its spirited charge.

First, it is well to recall the general outline of this early major engagement. McDowell, the Federal commander, advanced from the Washington defenses and undertook to turn the left flank of the army under Beauregard, the field commander of the Southern troops. By an early march on July 21, 1861, McDowell encircled the Confederate left. Beauregard by chance was massing his troops on his opposite flank to begin a like offense against the Federal left. The impetuous Federals drove in the weak Southern left flank, stormed up to the Henry House Hill and advanced the efficient Regular Army batteries of Ricketts and Griffin to the summit, where they pounded the Southern infantry brigades of Bee, Bartow, and Evans. The Confederate army was brought close to defeat.

Colonel Thomas Lanier Clingman, the North Carolinian who had just resigned from the United States Senate, and who as brigadier general later in the war would give an account of his gallantry at Petersburg and at the Weldon Railroad, was serving at Manassas on General Joseph E. Johnston's staff. He feared that the rapid firing of these batteries, augmenting the Northern musketry, would cause

the Confederate army to give way. Nearby Johnston was exclaiming, "If I had just three regiments! Just three regiments!"

But new factors were entering and soon Johnston and Beauregard would have much greater relief than expected. The stand of Stonewall Jackson, the arrival of fresh brigades from Johnston's Shenandoah Valley army, and the rally of the brigades of Bee, Bartow, and Evans turned the course of events sharply. Triumph came when Confederate troops, mainly the Sixth North Carolina of Bee's and Thirty-third Virginia of Stonewall Jackson's brigade, charged and captured the ten guns of Ricketts' and Griffin's batteries in the heart of the Federal position on Henry House Hill.

Clingman, with Johnston, watched an advancing regiment disappear into the pines, heard the crash of musketry and then only silence where before there had been a deep booming of the Northern cannon. The regiment was Colonel C. F. Fisher's Sixth North Carolina, a unit that would win even greater distinction storming and helping carry East Cemetery Hill at Gettysburg. One of its captains, later its colonel, Isaac E. Avery, who as commander of Hoke's brigade at Gettysburg would fall at the base of Cemetery Hill, jumped astride one of the six polished cannon that had been so tenderly cared for by the United States Regulars. As Clingman described the bloody affair, the Carolinians fired a volley, then finished off the artillerists with clubbed muskets and bowie knives. Knives and machete-type blades were not uncommon weapons in the early phases of the war. Ricketts was wounded and made prisoner. Scarcely had the guns been captured when Colonel Fisher fell from a bullet through his brain.

Fisher had been president of the North Carolina Railroad and had assembled the Sixth Regiment from among railroad workers and cadets volunteering from the North Carolina Military Institute at Charlotte. He brought them together in railroad barracks at the town known as Company Shops, now the City of Burlington. After the loss of Fisher, while the regiment was camping at Bristoe Station, it came under the command of one of North Carolina's greatest soldiers, Colonel William Dorsey Pender, Jeb Stuart's early friend and West Point classmate of 1854.

Other North Carolina regiments were in this first major campaign — the Fifth under Lieutenant Colonel Joseph P. Jones was part of Longstreet's brigade which at Blackburn's Ford met the first impact of McDowell's advance. The Twenty-first under Colonel W. W.

Battle Flag of the Sixth Regiment

Kirkland of Hillsboro served in the brigade of Brigadier General M. L. Bonham at Mitchell's Ford. Noble Twenty-first! This regiment fought in many of the great battles and served under some of the great names of American history — Ewell, Early, Pegram, Ramseur, Trimble, Hoke, Godwin, and Lewis. It was the regiment later commanded by Robert F. Hoke of Lincolnton. Hoke would rise from second lieutenant in the First Regiment to major general and eventually would become one of the best officers in Lee's army. Whispered was a tradition that emphasized his greatness. Lee himself had said late in the war, so the story went, that if he were killed or incapacitated for the command of the Army of Northern Virginia, he would rather see Robert Hoke assume it than any other man. The story has been challenged, of course, but there it is; and Lee could have made many less prudent choices.

From the Sixth Regiment's fighting at Manassas came the first story of how a Bible was supposed to have saved a soldier's life in battle, a coincidence that was repeated many times in the conflict. Willie Person Mangum, Jr., of Rougemont, Durham County, son of the former Whig Senator from North Carolina of that name, carried the Testament in his left coat pocket, a present from his sister. A bullet which hit the edge of the book was deflected sufficiently in its course to miss Mangum's heart. While the young man received a severe wound that crimsoned the Good Book with blood, the report went out from the battle that he was saved. He must have been hit again, or suffered later complications. A marker on the field of Manassas shows where he died.

The somber story of the barren Manassas campaign was summed up in a sentence by the chronicler of the Twenty-first North Carolina: "We pursued the enemy several miles, thinking we were going right into Washington, but were halted and ordered to retrace our steps."

Another who saw the possibilities of the field was a hitherto rather obscure brigade commander, recently professor of natural philosophy and artillery tactics, Thomas Jonathan Jackson. He could perceive that the highway to Washington and the possible termination of the war by a single stroke was as wide open as if strewn with welcoming garlands by McDowell's flying Zouaves.

Still, Stonewall Jackson's need for 10,000 fresh men — and there was ample allowance among those unengaged, including several North Carolina regiments — found President Davis arranging conferences, Johnston satisfied with the already gathered fruits of victory, and Beauregard concerned with rumors of advances on his rear. These rumors had phantom Union armies coming from all directions and seemed to cloud the fact that the flesh and blood Union army was fleeing double-quick toward the Potomac, followed no longer by even a squadron of cavalry. There were questions of supplies behind while flour was rotting in the freight cars and a rich country lay ahead.

Yet the elements of victory which fired Jackson's intuitive mind with the zest for further action spoke caution and satisfaction to his superiors, and the precious, wasted hours swept by. The Confederate army settled down for nine months almost on the spot, while the defenses of Washington were strengthened and a new Federal army was assembled.

Victory was a frequent visitor thereafter with the armies of the South, but the Northern volunteers who had raced from Bull Run hardened into stanch fighters; the attrition set in, and the war rolled on toward Gettysburg and Appomattox, with never another rout for the North so utter and complete, nor highway so clear, nor the cause of the South so near triumphant. And Jackson never had an opportunity to prove to history that, with 10,000 fresh men on the night of July 21, 1861, he would have been in Washington on the morrow.

MOUNTING HOPE AND HEAVY LOSS

In the grueling swamp battles of the Peninsula and on through Lee's bloody assault at Malvern Hill, North Carolina regiments were scattered among the commands of D. H. Hill, R. E. Colston, Richard S. Ewell, J. B. Magruder, James Longstreet, Theophilus H. Holmes, and A. P. Hill. In the succession of battles they were in front line action and at times in some of the most stubborn fighting of the war. Thus at Seven Pines the Fourth North Carolina lost in killed and wounded 24 officers and 462 enlisted men out of the 25 officers and 520 enlisted men it took into action, a casualty rate of 89 per cent. What rate is higher on any field, except at Thermopylae, the Alamo, or the massacre of the Swiss Guards? Every officer of the regiment except Major Bryan Grimes, who would rise to major general, was either killed or disabled.

Grimes, one of whose brigades fired the last shots at Appomattox, seemed to lead a charmed life in combat, only to fall from an assassin's bullet after the war while he was living at his quiet Pitt County retreat, "Grimesland."

What remained of the Fourth North Carolina after Seven Pines, and the recruits who joined it thereafter, became something of a darling among North State regiments insofar as clothing was concerned. The regiment had been organized at Camp Hill near Garysburg, in Northampton County, with George Burgwyn Anderson, a West Point graduate, as colonel and John Augustus Young, a textile manufacturer, as lieutenant colonel. Before Seven Pines, Young, in critical health, was sent home to procure uniforms. His illness disqualified him from further field duty. Vance set him to work making uniform cloth and he manufactured it at top energy in his plants until the end of the war. He never forgot the old Fourth. At his own expense, he provided every member with a brand new uniform and cap.

Heavy also was the loss of the Fifth North Carolina in its gallant charge at Williamsburg, made against the flanking brigade of Federal General Winfield Scott Hancock. Major James C. MacRae said of this movement that it "has rarely been surpassed in the history of war for its heroism and gallantry." The loss was 197 of the 240 engaged, or 82 per cent.

But such losses had to be sustained. Victory was riding high on Southern banners and the vast Federal army was being hurled back from Richmond. Hopes for independence mounted with each new triumph.

Youthful, high-spirited Zeb Vance, soon to be governor, commanded the Twenty-sixth North Carolina at Malvern Hill. Here the story was attributed to him (though told of other officers on other fields in other wars) that as he was advancing at the head of his men he stirred up a rabbit from the long grass and watched it bound

Major Bryan Grimes

frightened across the meadow ahead of the line. The soldiers hooted and urged it on.

"Go it, cotton tail," Vance shouted. "If I had no more reputation to lose than you have, I'd run, too."

That eased the tension of the tough assault. On this advance a bullet tore off the buttons and ripped open the jacket of Lieutenant Colonel John R. Lane of the Twenty-sixth. So tense was the moment that he did not remember he was carrying the regiment's pay, wrapped in a newspaper he had placed inside his blouse. When he recalled the money after the battle, it was gone. Lane, a bold officer who commanded this celebrated regiment in the later stages of the war, set out at once in search of the missing packet. McClellan's army had retreated, as had Lee's, but he did not know it. In the early morning light he walked back and forth among the dead bodies on the hillside, covering the bloody ground over which the regiment had attacked. There, finally, he espied the package, half-covered by some poor soldier's body, but still wrapped, tied and intact. What soldier did not rejoice, even after so desperate a combat, when he returned with the money that would mean food for near destitute families at home, or old sledge and poker cash for the more carefree in camp?

North Carolina was present also in Stonewall Jackson's campaign in the Shenandoah Valley, which Washington knew as the "Great

Scare." The State was represented by the Twenty-first Infantry Regiment in Isaac R. Trimble's brigade of Ewell's division. The brigade was in the lead in the sharp repulse of the Federal General Freemont at Cross Keys. Trimble complimented the Twenty-first for its conduct.

One of the quirks of fate occurred in the Twenty-first Regiment at the fiercely fought battle of Winchester, where Stonewall Jackson defeated Federal General Banks. There Captain John W. Beard of Company F was riddled with enemy bullets. Eight minié balls tore through his body, several of them into his bowels, yet to the amazement of the doctors and to all the known laws of the world of violence, he survived the battle, the war, and even the nineteenth century, and was living hale and happily in Kansas when Major James F. Beall wrote his sketch of the regiment in 1901.

North Carolina suffered two severe losses in the battles around Richmond. Colonel Montford S. Stokes of the First Regiment was killed at Beaver Dam on June 26, 1862, in the first of the Seven Days' Battles. Colonel Gaston Meares of the Third Regiment fell at Malvern Hill. Both were widely known and honored in the State and in Lee's army.

Chapter

NORTH TO ANTIETAM CREEK

PAST CEDAR MOUNTAIN and Second Manassas North Carolinians marched and fought in Lee's army in the full flush of victory until they reached the bloody field of Sharpsburg (Antietam), the culmination of Lee's first venture north of the Potomac. The battle was brought on by a lost order involving either Lee's couriers or North Carolina General D. H. Hill or his staff. The incident occurred after the army vacated Frederick, Maryland, where it had concentrated after crossing the Potomac. Because of their high significance to the campaign and the war, as well as their relation to the ranking North Carolina general in Lee's army, the events should be related briefly.

First, the campaign. Of the two thrusts made by the Army of Northern Virginia into the North, climaxing in battles at Sharpsburg and Gettysburg, opinion persisted among some of Lee's generals, and notably Longstreet, that the conditions of invasion were the more promising in the Sharpsburg campaign. Had not Lee divided his army in the presence of the enemy, and had not McClellan been apprised of that division by a freak of circumstance, the South would have had an excellent prospect to win a major engagement on Union soil, which might have secured Maryland to the Confederacy. It is remotely possible it might have obtained the required recognition by European powers. So this line of reasoning went. But Lee did divide his army, and McClellan learned of the division through one of those queer casts of chance.

Lee led across the Potomac a highly efficient, veteran force, small in numbers for an extended movement, but responsive to his wishes and comprising possibly the best fighting unit he ever had. It possessed the prestige of repeated victory and numbered not second among its many elements of strength the talented and energetic commander of the Second Corps, Jackson. And by the time of Gettysburg, when Lee had his other opportunity for invasion, Stonewall Jackson already had passed across the river and was resting under the shade of the trees.

Certain it is that the campaign in Maryland was frustrated by one of those minor coincidences which often shape the destinies of people at moments of stress and trial. As McClellan's army, following Lee northward by easy stages, pitched camp at Frederick, Williams' division occupied ground which D. H. Hill's division, of Jackson's corps, had just left. Private B. W. Mitchell of Muncie, Indiana, Company F, Twenty-seventh Indiana Volunteer Infantry, noticed on the ground, while stacking arms, a paper wrapper encircling three cigars tied with a bit of string. Paper was a matter of indifference, but cigars were something to be reckoned with in any Federal army. But Private Mitchell examined the paper and his eyes almost bulged from their sockets when he noted its contents. Rushing to First Sergeant Bloss he disclosed his find, and the two made haste to Colonel Silas Colgrove, commanding the regiment. Colgrove, equally excited, lost no time in going to the tent of General A. S. Williams, where he delivered the prized document to Colonel S. E. Pittman, divisional adjutant. Pittman took it directly to McClellan, who was fully as agitated as Colonel Pittman, Colonel Colgrove, Sergeant Bloss, or Private Mitchell.

It was an original copy, signed and attested, of Lee's orders to the Army of Northern Virginia, revealing on its face how he had divided his two wings and detailing the routes over which the different elements of his army were moving. One, Jackson's, went back to Harper's Ferry; the other, Longstreet's, went on toward Hagerstown. Such a separation of forces in the face of the Federal advance was hazardous even under conditions of top secrecy. The disclosure might easily spell disaster. So obvious was this that some of Lee's generals took extraordinary precaution against losing their copies. Walker pinned his to the inside of his pocket. Longstreet read his until he knew it thoroughly and then put his copy into his mouth and chewed it.

Enterprise by scouts, spies, vedettes, patrols, and cavalry and infantry reconnaissances could scarcely have possessed the Union commander with information so authentic and valuable. The order had been issued by Lee's headquarters to General D. H. Hill. It bore the signature of Colonel R. H. Chilton, Lee's adjutant general, which Colonel Pittman instantly recognized as genuine from his familiarity with Chilton's writing in the old army before the war. Hill received his regular copy of the order from his corps commander, Jackson, and had it years later as proof that he had not been dilatory. Lee's staff must have issued an individual copy for Hill direct, without sending it through routine channels, and possibly this copy found employment as a cigar wrapper and thereby attracted Private Mitchell's notice. The matter of how it was lost has been subject to dispute which many have attempted without success to clear, and some on Lee's staff always held Hill accountable. But surely enough, on the afternoon of September 13, 1862, McClellan had an authentic copy of Special Order No. 191, of Lee's army.

Unusual haste and bustle were now apparent in McClellan's slow moving army, for fate had handed to its commander a rare opportunity. Within two hours after the finding of the order, which was breath-taking speed as things had gone with McClellan on the Peninsula, he had a division on the march toward South Mountain, where

the seizure of one of the passes and a prompt movement by the remaining divisions would have meant an interposition of his forces between Lee's separate wings at Harper's Ferry and Hagerstown, twenty-five miles apart. McClellan had twice as large an army as Lee, and the latter was in the unfortunate condition of having Jackson and Longstreet on opposite sides of the Potomac.

While the tornado was forming itself in Lee's rear, another element entered the drama to give his army a soothing breath of life. A sympathetic Marylander had overheard the hubbub in McClellan's tent when the lost dispatch was brought to the Union general, and recognizing the extraordinary importance of this disclosure, mounted promptly and rode through the night the distance to Hagerstown, where Lee was advised that his order was the property of McClellan.

With Lee informed, everything was action. D. H. Hill was directed to the defense of Turner's Gap and Longstreet was rushed to his assistance. Messengers flew to McLaws and Jackson, urging haste at Harper's Ferry, where the Union garrison was surrounded and captured. Hill and Longstreet would delay McClellan at South Mountain, and the concentration would be effected at Sharpsburg, which was virtually the only point on the map where Lee could join his two wings and still keep his army in Maryland. He did not want to retire to Virginia ignominiously without a battle.

D. H. Hill's thin gray line held at Turner's Gap as Longstreet rushed from Hagerstown. Lee retired to Sharpsburg, with his left wing reduced to scarcely more than 15,000, there to await Jackson. These were anxious hours for Lee. But McClellan was tardy and Jackson fast.

Jackson arrived after an all-night march and Lee drew his lines behind Antietam Creek. The Potomac River rolled in his immediate rear. Hooker, the most dashing of the Union corps commanders, attacked on the late afternoon of September 16, 1862. The battle of Antietam opened with full fury on the next morning. That the battle was fought on the terms of the Federals was the price Lee paid for the lost order. He was fortunate, due to McClellan's slowness, to be able to fight with his army united.

Chapter VII

A CAROLINA BRIGADE HOLDS THE "BLOODY LANE"

THE BATTLE along Antietam Creek was the most sanguinary of any single day's action on the soil of the two Americas. No other day took such toll from both sides. The armies of the North and the South looked upon this as the deciding moment.

Often during the day the cause of the Confederacy wavered, as Northern youths threw themselves in masses of brigades and divisions into the East Wood, into the West Wood, into the wood at the Dunker Church, into Mumma's farm, into Roulette's farm, into the Piper farm, and into the sunken road known always thereafter as the "Bloody Lane."

If North Carolina were at fault in bringing on the battle under unfavorable conditions, the North State troops compensated by the ardor of their fighting. However his staff may have been involved in the lost order, if at all, D. H. Hill cleaned the slate by his dogged defense of the town of Sharpsburg in the center of Lee's position. To lose Sharpsburg would undoubtedly have been to lose the battle and the war.

The name indelibly associated with Sharpsburg is the "Bloody Lane," the sunken zigzag roadway in front of Lee's center, where D. H. Hill's division and mainly the brigade of George B. Anderson, composed of the Second, Fourth, Fourteenth, and Thirtieth North Carolina Regiments, obstinately battled the Federal division commanded in turn by Major General Israel B. Richardson and, when he was mortally wounded, by Brigadier General Winfield Scott Hancock. In few if any instances of the war was the fighting more sanguinary than along this little dirt roadway, heaped with the dead of both armies.

Here Anderson — "as brave and daring as a man could be" — was mortally wounded. Born near Hillsboro, he attended both the University of North Carolina and West Point, and was graduated from the Military Academy in 1852. When he resigned his commission to espouse the Confederate cause he was a first lieutenant of dragoons. He became colonel of the Fourth North Carolina, showed himself to be a fierce, determined fighter, and won his general's rank on the Peninsula. The ball he received at Sharpsburg amounted to no more than a foot wound. The foot had to be amputated and he died from the surgery a month after the battle. He was thirty-two years old. His brigade would be led later with high distinction by General Stephen Dodson Ramseur. It came to be called the "Ironsides of the Army."

Colonel C. C. Tew of the Second North Carolina was killed outright. Nothing in the later history of this North State brigade, which under Ramseur executed the brilliant turning movement that helped to dislodge the Federal army on July 1 north and west of Gettysburg, and which fought heroically on many other fields, surpassed its tenacious stand in the center of the line at Sharpsburg.

When the returns were finally in, it could be seen that the heaviest loss suffered by any brigade in either army was that of Colonel Van H. Manning's brigade of Brigadier General John G. Walker's division, composed largely of North Carolina troops. It consisted of the Twenty-seventh, Forty-sixth and Forty-eighth North Carolina Regiments, along with the Third Arkansas and Thirtieth Virginia. Fighting mainly in the center, alongside Brigadier General Robert Ransom's brigade, also of Walker's division and also from North Carolina, Manning's casualties numbered 140 killed, 684 wounded, and 93 missing, a total of 917. Apparently the second highest brigade loss was that of the Federal Napoleon J. T. Dana's brigade of John Sedgwick's division, which was cut to pieces in the Miller cornfield, where it suffered casualties of 142 killed, 652 wounded, and 104 missing, a total of 898. Manning's brigade fought with Anderson's along the "Bloody Lane."

One of its regiments, the Twenty-seventh North Carolina, was commanded in this action by Colonel John Rogers Cooke, "Jeb" Stuart's brother-in-law and son of the well-known cavalry officer of the old army, General Philip St. George Cooke, who had remained with the Union. The Confederate Colonel Cooke's rejoinder to Longstreet during the battle involved a deal of profanity but did show the spirit of the Twenty-seventh North Carolina. When Longstreet saw how well the single regiment was maintaining its position, which, he said, should have been held by from four to six brigades, he sent his Chief of Staff G. Moxley Sorrel to commend the colonel and tell him to continue to hold firm. Cooke thanked him and sent back this reply: "But say, by God almighty, he needn't doubt me. We'll stay here, by Jesus Christ, if we must all go to hell together." That, at any rate, was the way Sorrel worded the message. The more restrained Longstreet had Cooke say merely that "he would show his colors as long as there was a man alive to hold them up."

Other North Carolina units fought nobly along the bloody Antietam. Brigadier General Lawrence O'Bryan Branch, who in his forty-two years already had so established himself in the law and in Congress that he had been offered two posts in President Buchanan's cabinet (the Treasury and Post Office) was killed. Branch had led his men with high distinction in North Carolina battles and in A. P. Hill's Light Division on the Peninsula. His brigade, later commanded by James H. Lane, under whom it marched in the Pickett-Pettigrew-

Brigadier General
Lawrence O'Bryan Branch

Trimble assault at Gettysburg, had won from Stonewall Jackson a tribute perhaps unsurpassed in the war. It had performed so nobly under Branch at Cedar Run, filling the hole when the celebrated Stonewall Brigade had been driven back, that on parade after the battle Jackson had ridden to it. He used no words to express his thanks — and thanks of any nature were not dispensed lightly by Jackson. He merely doffed his quaint little private's cap that was his favorite headgear and dropped it to the ground in front of the North Carolinians. Whimsical are the plays of fate. The fire of one of the regiments of this brigade would wound Jackson mortally at Chancellorsville.

One of the small, enlightening incidents at Sharpsburg indicative of Stonewall Jackson's boldness involved an enlisted man named Hood of the Thirty-fifth North Carolina, commanded by Colonel Matt W. Ransom, later the distinguished North Carolina Senator and "father" of Potomac Park in Washington. The Colonel's brother, Brigadier General Robert Ransom, commanded the brigade, a part of Walker's division.

Though Lee fought Sharpsburg with something less than 40,000 men, against McClellan's near 90,000, Jackson, who commanded Lee's left, conceived, with a boldness which would have been accounted rashness in a less able performer, the notion that he might turn the Federal right flank, roll it up along Antietam Creek and capture the better part of McClellan's army. Perhaps he was inspired by his capture a few days earlier of the Federal garrison of Harper's Ferry, whose commander lifted the white flag after scarcely firing a shot.

When the fighting lagged in the afternoon after McClellan's vicious but piecemeal attacks on Lee's left and center, Jackson rode along the line of the North Carolinians and told Colonel Ransom of his hope — more than that, his intention — to encircle the hostile flank and reach McClellan's rear. But he wanted an impression of the forces opposing him and sent Hood clambering up a tall tree to get a look at the enemy reserves behind the East Woods, the clump of timber from which the Federals had launched their early attack. Jackson called up and inquired how many bluecoats Hood could see.

"Who-e-e!" Hood shouted down. "There are oceans of them, General."

"Count their flags," commanded Jackson.

Hood spent some time checking the horizon and told Jackson he could see thirty-nine flags. That was too many hostile regiments, even for Jackson. His hope of a turning movement was abandoned. More about who this North Carolina soldier was, whose count kept Lee's small army wisely on the defensive, the record does not say; but there were two Hoods among the enlisted men on the roster of the Thirty-fifth. They were Corporal Benjamin F. Hood of Henderson County in Company G and Private John R. Hood of Mecklenburg County in Company H.

Lee's right was so thinly held behind Antietam Creek that when the Federal General Burnside finally crossed at the bridge which now bears his name, the Confederate army was brought close to disaster. At this juncture in the afternoon, A. P. Hill's Light Division, heavy with North Carolina regiments in the brigades of Branch and the able Brigadier General William Dorsey Pender, reached the field after a grueling forced march from Harper's Ferry, arriving at the moment of high crisis to the Confederate cause. In fifteen minutes it would have been too late. Hill threw his division against Burnside's loose flank. The movement was brilliant and sufficient. Burnside was rolled back in confusion.

Night finally came, and with it the evidence of the greatest carnage that marked the fratricidal war in America. Among the dead were many of the most intrepid officers of the two armies. Fifteen generals had been struck down. Of the 105,000 engaged of the two armies, out of 130,000 on the field, 21,000 were killed or wounded. The losses of Ewell's old division were 47 per cent. And these troops had been on the defensive. McClellan's grand army was cut to shreds. He called urgently on Halleck for reinforcements, depicting the emergency of his situation.

Lee met his generals that night in the Grove House in Sharpsburg. An indication of the battle is seen from Hood's reply, when Lee asked him the location of his division. "They are lying on the field, where you sent them." Any other man probably would have regarded his case as hopeless, but Lee finally concluded, "If McClellan wants to fight in the morning, I will give him battle."

McClellan, on the morning of September 18, was not anxious to resume the attack. The beautiful day of the early Maryland autumn wore on, with an occasional artillery shot, and the two crimsoned armies stood face to face.

Nobody knew whether either had won a victory. The blue and gray lines glared at each other from the Dunker Church, the West Wood, the East Wood, the Mumma farm and the Roulette farm, and along the "Bloody Lane."

But as the late afternoon shadows lengthened into dusk, the invading General came to understand that the story of the Maryland liberation was ended. That night the artillery caissons rolled toward the Potomac. By morning Lee's army was on the Virginia shore.

Thus was fought and thus ended one of the most vast and deadly battles of North Carolina and Confederate history, ranking with Gettysburg and Chickamauga in desperate, costly combat on every acre of the field.

THE EIGHTEENTH NORTH CAROLINA'S FATAL VOLLEY

THE ANGUISH OF ANTIETAM was followed by Fredericksburg, a battle the Northern army never should have fought. Again was North Carolina in the forefront of the deadly fray. Burnside hurled his Grand Divisions against Lee's well-nigh impregnable position on Marye's Heights and darkened the plain with the blue-clad bodies of the dead.

Lee's losses were moderate, compared with Burnside's, but one-third of the Confederates who went down were from North Carolina.

Fredericksburg and the "Mud March," on which the Federal army mired itself in red clay in a northern Virginia winter, ended Burnside and gave the army to the often brilliant, at times lethargic, altogether erratic Hooker. When the spring of 1863 came to Virginia and the cowslip and violet showed themselves and the dogwood blossomed in the forest, "Fighting Joe" Hooker led his reorganized army, more than double Lee's in strength, into the thickets around Chancellorsville. By the audacious celerity of his movement, he threatened to bypass Lee, who was weakened by the absence of most of Longstreet's corps, and gain the high road to Richmond.

Brilliant was Hooker's strategy and bold was the answer devised by Lee and Jackson at their celebrated night council, held sitting on cracker boxes before a fire of pine twigs in the woods. Numerous North Carolina units participated in Jackson's hazardous march by which he turned Hooker's right flank, much as Hooker had sought to turn Lee's. The Thirtieth North Carolina of Ramseur's brigade was in the lead as Jackson felt his way along the circuitous trails. When the celebrated Stonewall formed his command for his demolishing blow, with Rodes' division in the first line, Colston's in the second, and A. P. Hill's in the third, nineteen veteran North Carolina regiments were in the attacking group.

Falling like a tornado on the Eleventh Federal Corps, which composed Hooker's right and which was made up mainly of German immigrants, Jackson's men rolled up the flank and hurled what remained of it back on the Federal center huddled around the Chancellorsville clearing and farmhouse. The Germans rushed back with alarmed cries of "Shackson! Shackson!" The strategy was Lee's; the tactics were Jackson's masterpiece.

Here, as at Antietam, Jackson was intent on the possibility of encircling the Federal army and capturing as goodly a portion of it as he could. That earnest purpose led to one of the grievous episodes of North Carolina and Confederate history, the fatal wounding of Jackson by a volley from the Eighteenth North Carolina Regiment of Lane's brigade.

No other volley of the war had so profound a bearing on the fortunes of the South; yet such were the circumstances that none could attach blame to the North State troops who fired it.

Lane's brigade of A. P. Hill's division, in the third line when Jackson struck, was passed to the front when the initial impetus of the first two lines was spent. Hill's division was then ordered to renew the advance. Lane's brigade straddled the Plank Road, down which Jackson's flank assault was being delivered. Night had fallen as Lane got into position. About him were the jumbled masses of the two armies, disorganized in the darkness. Two of Lane's regiments, the Eighteenth and Twenty-eighth North Carolina, were on the left side of the Plank Road, the Eighteenth with its right resting on the roadway. Dense growths of scrub oak made visibility and maneuver difficult. Ahead, one of Lane's regiments, the Thirty-third North Carolina, was deployed as skirmishers. Such was the setting for the great tragedy of the war.

En route to ask Hill about the attack orders, Lane encountered Jackson, his old Virginia Military Institute professor, who recognized his voice as he was calling for Hill. Jackson's tone was "earnest," as Lane described it. He gestured toward the enemy with his right hand. "Push right ahead, Lane," he ordered, then rode on in the darkness.

Lane moved to the right. The armies were so tangled together that at this juncture a Pennsylvania colonel appeared behind Lane's skirmishers and came to the firing line holding aloft a stick with a white handkerchief. All he wanted was to satisfy his curiosity. He inquired whether Lane's troops were friends or foes, which he learned by being taken prisoner. Just then Lane heard a burst of small arms firing. Soon Pender, who had taken command of the division, rode up, suspended the attack, and gave the information that Stonewall Jackson had gone down in front of his own men. Then Lane learned that A. P. Hill had been wounded in the same blast.

What had happened was that Jackson, after leaving Lane, had rejoined his staff and with A. P. Hill and Hill's staff had ridden forward to reconnoiter. Colonel Clark M. Avery of the Thirty-third North Carolina, the skirmishers out in front, had seen the generals pass ahead of the skirmish line and had warned his men against pushing forward on the attack before they returned. Suddenly the Federal lines in front of the skirmishers erupted with rifle and artillery fire, directed mainly along the Plank Road. It was after nine o'clock and the woods were in utter darkness.

Jackson and his party came dashing back at a gallop. They passed safely through the skirmish line of the Thirty-third Regiment. They inclined to the right of the road to avoid the artillery fire, which was concentrated on the roadway. This threw them into the dark, thick woods. Just after they had passed, the skirmishers heard a shout in the rear, coming from the line of the Eighteenth Regiment. Someone was calling out, "Yankee cavalry!" Then came a burst of musketry. With bullets tearing the air about them from both front and rear, the skirmishers hit the dirt. A short time later they had word that the firing they escaped by dropping to the ground had brought down Jackson.

The size of Jackson's party was what led to the fatal error. As Captain Alfred H. H. Tolar of Company L, Eighteenth North Carolina, who witnessed the incident, pointed out, thirty horsemen crashing rapidly through the heavy woods might readily be mistaken by infantrymen for a whole brigade of cavalry. Nobody in the Eighteenth had been advised that a reconnoitering party had gone out in front. In the darkness Jackson and the others had passed down the Plank Road slowly and unnoticed. Lane had alerted his entire brigade by telling them they composed the front line of the Confederate army and should be attentive to everything in their front. When a group of horsemen came charging down on them it was natural that they should expect enemies and greet the oncomers as such.

Colonel Thomas J. Purdie, who commanded the Eighteenth, heard the advance of the horsemen and told his men to fix bayonets. Then, when the party was about 100 yards in his front, he issued the fatal order, "Commence firing!" The volley shattered the night air. It was followed by sustained firing — "with great rapidity," according to Captain Tolar — from the entire regiment. Even when one of the mounted party shouted that the North Carolinians were firing on friends, it seemed so incredible that it was disbelieved. An officer shouted that it was a lie. Only when Arthur S. Smith of Company K knocked down a horse with his gun butt and thereby dismounted one of Jackson's staff officers, was the truth finally established.

Jackson fell at the first burst of heavy fire. Because the volley was general it was out of the question to determine who might have fired the fatal bullet. But none in the Eighteenth ever sought to place the blame on any other regiment. As Captain Tolar stated, no shots were heard from any other troops. Colonel Purdie was killed in the battle and left no account; but Major John D. Barry, later colonel of the Regiment, whom Lane described as "one of my bravest and most ac-

General Stonewall Jackson

complished officers," accepted full responsibility and said he had ordered the firing and had declared the cry that they were firing on friends to be a lie. In the palpable blackness who could know he was blazing away at his beloved commander, the cold genius Stonewall?

Chief Justice Walter Clark of the North Carolina Supreme Court, who as editor and compiler gave to his State and to posterity the five monumental volumes entitled ***Histories of the Several Regiments and Battalions from North Carolina in the Great War,*** *1861-65,* made some observations on the heavy loss the South suffered on that night of Lee's victory at Chancellorsville. There fell in his prime, the Chief Justice said, "the greatest soldier the war produced. . . ." What heights he might have reached could not be known, "for he was constantly growing." Then Judge Clark dwelt on the capriciousness of fate.

"It is a singular reflection that notwithstanding the countless tons of bullets, cannon balls and shell fired during those four eventful years, two minié balls, in all human probability, decided the result. . . . The bullet that slew Albert Sidney Johnston when in another hour he would have captured the Western Army with Grant and Sherman at its head and that other bullet which prostrated 'Stonewall' Jackson when on the eve of capturing Hooker's army destroyed our hopes of success." He quoted in his concluding verdict the remark of Napier on Napoleon: *"Fortune, that name for the unknown combinations of an infinite power,* was wanting to us and without her aid, the designs of man are as bubbles upon a troubled ocean."

Those who believe the outcome of the war depended on mass and not inspiration, who saw victory in Northern industry and not in military leadership, who accept Wellington's dictum that God fights on the side of the heavy battalion, will demur from Judge Clark's opinion. But who knows? Stonewall had accomplished so much with so little. And all must agree with Judge Clark that he was "constantly growing."

Chapter IX

REINFORCEMENTS FROM NORTH CAROLINA

LIKE PYRRHUS after Asuculum and Hannibal after Cannae, Lee was rich with victories in the late spring of 1863, but independence, the Southern objective, was no nearer to realization than when the states seceded. Desperate measures were imperative, else the South would bleed itself out in triumphs.

Early 1863, in fact, had been a season of despondency. Food shortages and high prices had led to rioting, mainly by a mob of Richmond women. Some contended that the looting and tumult had been prearranged by Northern agents. Commanding a martial nation that had become almost an armed camp, both President Jefferson Davis and Secretary of War James Alexander Seddon were unmilitary in mental posture and physically emaciated and unhealthy for their trying duties in such troubled times. Davis, learned, scholarly and resolute, but with rigid thought patterns, feeble constitution and poor eyesight, labored incessantly. Overloaded with work, he was easily agitated. Seddon, formerly a Virginia congressman, was so sallow that he was said at the War Department, over which he presided, to "resemble an exhumed corpse after a month's interment."

Above the frailty of the officials and the miserable weather of early 1863, or the food shortages and high prices, or the indifference of foreign powers to Confederate needs for recognition, the Southern people — and North Carolina at the very forefront — suffered most grievously from the appalling casualty lists. More than one-third of Lee's battle dead and one-fourth of the wounded in the Chancellorsville campaign were North Carolina troops, though the State supplied only twenty-five of the regiments and separate battalions of the 129 in Lee's army, or roughly one-fifth of the battle force.

In this season a somber hush seemed to settle over the South. The measured march of the funeral procession was heard again and again in the city streets, a wail of anguish pitched to the temper of the cold, reluctant spring. Each time the invaders were repelled they crowded in again. War, as always, was proving not so much pageantry and glory as heart-tearing sacrifice. "It seems that we are never out of the sound of the Dead March. . . . It comes and it comes, until I feel inclined to close my eyes and scream."

At last, on May 12, the plaintive strain sounded with deepest poignancy. The cortege that moved through the Richmond streets was that of Stonewall Jackson himself. President Davis, "thin and frail," led the procession on foot, followed by the Cabinet, headed by the serene, unfathomable Judah P. Benjamin, Secretary of State. Cadaverous Secretary of War Seddon was behind him and files of distinguished generals served as pallbearers. "Little Sorrel," Stonewall's faithful horse, was led by a servant. Again Richmond was shocked by the silent testimony of the empty saddle. The newly designed, near-white banner of the Confederate States that draped Jackson's coffin could scarcely be seen beneath the masses of snow-white May blossoms, and there was grief in his Charlotte, North Carolina, home. The body lay in state at the Capitol. Hour after hour the people passed the bier and gazed through the glass-covered aperture on the peaceful, resolute countenance of one of the great captains of history.

But summer came, the harvest was at hand in the Gulf Coast states, Lee was assembling his scattered forces, and the buoyancy of the army that was restored after Chancellorsville gave new promise to the home public. Youth is confident and faces forward. Lee had bold plans, and the army was on the move. Among the inspiring factors was more help from North Carolina, which sent up two fresh brigades that could be spared from the coastal defense in the urgency of the Commanding General's intention to invade the Northern states.

These were the all-North Carolina brigades of Brigadier General James Johnston Pettigrew and Brigadier General Junius Daniel. Another addition was the brigade of Joseph R. Davis from the Richmond defenses. It contained a single North Carolina regiment, the Fifty-fifth, destined for high distinction on the heights at Gettysburg.

It was a coincidence that these three brigades — Pettigrew's, Daniel's and Davis' — containing troops which were to be contemptuously and erroneously referred to as "raw troops" in some newspaper accounts and historical works on the invasion of Pennsylvania, suffered the heaviest losses in battle deaths among all the brigades of Lee's army at Gettysburg. Raw troops, indeed! Lee could have used many more like them.

Except for some mild dissents involving special pleading for especially favored battles, it is generally conceded that the Confederate cause reached its high point of opportunity at Gettysburg. This story about North Carolina in the war is not intended as a general account of the battle. Many histories can be found elsewhere telling how Southern fortunes rose and fell on that field; how chance often seemed to control the critical deployments, evolutions and actions; how delays, at times costly, at times fortuitous, took capricious control over events; how the battle moved indecisively but inexorably toward the tragic climax of the Pickett-Pettigrew-Trimble assault; and how after that repulse and a day of inaction on the field, while the heavens unloosed a downpour, Lee finally and reluctantly came to an understanding that the Northern army could not be dislodged, and began the long retreat that continued beyond the Wilderness thickets and the Petersburg trenches to Appomattox.

Substantially all North Carolina units performed outstanding service in this desperately fought battle, but at least three regiments are entitled to especial mention here because of the notable manner in which they answered their unusual opportunities on that field. They may be used to symbolize the type of soldiers and the nature of the performance the State gave to Lee's army.

The Eleventh North Carolina, of Pettigrew's brigade, established the initial contact with the Federals and suffered perhaps the second highest casualties of any of Lee's regiments. The Eleventh might claim it was the senior battle regiment of the army because it was the reorganized "Bethel Regiment," which Hill had commanded in the first noteworthy engagement of the war.

Probably no regiment in the Southern service possessed a commander better qualified to train and lead it than did the Eleventh. Colonel Collett Leventhorpe, scion of a wealthy and knightly family of Devonshire, England, had been educated at Winchester College and commissioned an ensign in the Forty-fourth Regiment of British Foot, the regiment which, incidentally, though well before his service in it, occupied and burned Washington in the War of 1812. He had traveled about the world, served in the British army in the West Indies, Canada and Ireland, and had risen to the rank of captain, but had decided to emigrate to the United States and study medicine.

After graduating with honors at Charleston, South Carolina, he established his practice in Rutherfordton, the western North Carolina town that had flourished after gold had been discovered and a mint was set up in 1831. Through the succeeding eighteen years, memories of crimson uniforms and the dull exactions of garrison drill dimmed amid life and service in the glorious surroundings of the Blue Ridge foothills. When North Carolina seceded and the young men of Rutherford County hurried forward and formed companies, the fervor of his adopted people in their battle for independence stirred again the martial spirit of this old British soldier. Although he was then forty-six years old, he stepped out with the North State youths. When the new Eleventh Regiment was organized, made up of recruits and the veterans of the early First Volunteers, he quite understandably was elected colonel. The lieutenant colonel was the warmly admired professor of mineralogy at the University of North Carolina, William J. Martin.

The half-forgotten days in the British army now crowded back on Colonel Leventhorpe, and he soon was looked upon as "probably the best finished and equipped field officer in the Confederate service." The Eleventh was representative of a strip running across the State, from the heart of the hills through the Piedmont to Bertie County, washed by the waters of Albemarle Sound. It trained chiefly at Wilmington and developed such precision that the Colonel could offer no other criticism than that it was "not quite as proficient as British regulars." Yet such was grudging praise indeed, compared with the glowing words of the Inspector General of the Confederate Army, R. H. Chilton. He reported to General Lee, when the organization was incorporated in Lee's army, that "the Eleventh Regiment of North Carolina troops is the best drilled, the best equipped and the best armed regiment in the Army of Northern Virginia."

We have seen Pettigrew's second regiment, the Twenty-sixth North Carolina Infantry, which had been Governor Vance's regiment, as it charged up Malvern Hill. Its company names showed it was raised largely from the Piedmont: the Chatham Boys, Moore Independents, Caldwell Guards, Pee Dee Wildcats; but two companies of hill men were among them — the Wilkes Volunteers from the

Colonel Harry King Burgwyn

region of Deep Gap and the slopes of Rendezvous Mountain, and the Jeff Davis Mountaineers, from Ashe County in the northwest corner of the State. Company B, the "Hornet's Nest Rifles" of Charlotte — a town famous as the "Hornet's Nest" in Revolutionary War times — had suffered the first war casualty in the death of Private James Hudson, though he had died from natural causes and not in battle.

The Twenty-sixth had come to vie with the Eleventh as "the best drilled regiment." Its pride was Captain Mickey's ornate regimental band, which an unnamed member of the regiment declared was "considered the finest in the Army of Northern Virginia." One thing obviously was not lacking. The regiment had an admirable *esprit de corps.*

After Vance was elected governor the regiment was commanded by Colonel Harry King Burgwyn, an honor graduate of the University of North Carolina and later a student under Jackson at the Virginia Military Institute. Though he was known as the "boy colonel" and was only twenty-one years old at the time of Gettysburg, he was a highly gifted leader who possessed the affection and confidence of his men. This was well manifested when the better part of the regiment — 82 per cent according to North Carolina returns — laid down their lives with him during Pettigrew's sanguinary attack against the "Iron Brigade" of the Federal army on the first day on McPherson Heights west of Gettysburg.

There the Twenty-sixth North Carolina engaged in the most deadly regimental duel of the battle. It encountered mainly the Twenty-fourth Michigan of the "Iron Brigade." The Michigan regiment was commanded by Colonel Henry A. Morrow, a native of Virginia who as a boy had moved to Detroit. The two regiments fought until few remained on either side. One of Burgwyn's companies, recruited from the Grandfather Mountain area and commanded by Captain R. M. Tuttle, who later became a Presbyterian minister, had every one of its eighty-eight enlisted men and three officers either killed or wounded. In another company, two were untouched out of eighty-two engaged. Still another went in with ninety-two and came out with fifteen fit for service.

Colonel Burgwyn was killed at the head of his regiment. His men buried him that night with a gun case for a coffin, beneath a large walnut tree where he fell, on the crest of the ridge where the remnants of his regiment finally drove the few Michigan survivors back toward Gettysburg.

Both the Eleventh and Twenty-sixth North Carolina Regiments were in Pettigrew's brigade of Harry Heth's division, A. P. Hill's corps. The other of the three regiments that should be signaled out as typifying the high spirit and gallant performance of the Old North State units was the Fifty-fifth North Carolina, of Joseph R. Davis' brigade, Heth's division. This regiment made the farthest advance against the Federal lines on Cemetery Hill in the justly celebrated Pickett-Pettigrew-Trimble assault — known as Longstreet's assault or more often erroneously as "Pickett's charge" — on the afternoon of July 3. It gave to North Carolina the second phase of the State's treasured motto, "Farthest at Gettysburg."

The Fifty-fifth, a newcomer to Lee's army, had taken advantage of its opportunities to drill in a quiet sector of the North Carolina seacoast. It was distinctly a young man's regiment, not an officer and very likely not a soldier in it having attained the age of thirty. Colonel John Kerr Connally of Yadkin County had given evidence of his spirit when the regiment came into contact with Longstreet's corps during the siege of Suffolk, while the intrepid Major A. H. Belo, a principal in the same incident, was described as "a fine specimen of young Southern manhood."

At Suffolk, shortly before marching to join General Lee, the Fifty-fifth had been occupied for a time with matters as pressing as meeting the Federal army. Federal troops had made a sudden and disconcerting descent and captured a heavy piece of artillery. In making their report of the incident, two officers of Law's Alabama brigade, Hood's division — Captain L. R. Terrell, assistant adjutant general, and Captain John Cussons, an English-born scout of Law's staff — stated that the Fifty-fifth North Carolina had been assigned to protect the piece, but had retired in an unbecoming manner. The Fifty-fifth was in no manner accountable, according to its officers, and had maintained its position and yielded no ground. The incensed Colonel Connally, stirred by what he regarded a grave injustice, promptly called on Law and then on Law's staff members and demanded that they correct their report at once. Possibly because they were confronted with such a show of anger — Connally had called the report "a damned lie" — they declined to do so.

Connally returned to his regiment and summoned all field officers and captains to an urgent meeting. He insisted that the honor of the

regiment was offended. This point seemed obvious to the other officers. None appeared to think of appealing to higher authority in order that the facts might be investigated and the report corrected. The Colonel, who was twenty-six years old, proposed that the two ranking field officers of the regiment should challenge the two Alabamians, and that if they did not obtain satisfaction or if they were killed, the other officers in turn should take up the issue until satisfaction had been received or the regiment's last officer had been killed.

Colonel Connally challenged Captain Terrell, and Major Belo challenged Captain Cussons. The Alabamians quite gladly accepted. Captain Terrell made a choice of weapons that would have caused the most punctilious Southerner to lift his eyebrows. He specified double-barreled shotguns loaded with buckshot. Somebody was very likely to be killed. The other Alabamian, Captain Cussons, chose Mississippi rifles at forty paces. Excitement ran through the army but the high officers looked elsewhere. Belo and Cussons came to their places and took the positions their seconds assigned, shouldered their rifles and fired. Belo's aim was good, but the bullet only grazed his adversary's head and ripped through his hat. Cussons, either from bad aim or intent, missed entirely. Very likely the miss caused Belo on his second shot to fire wide. Cussons' second bullet tore through Belo's uniform just above the shoulder.

Meanwhile friends of both Connally and Terrell were attempting a reconciliation. The matter of the original criticism of the Fifty-fifth Regiment was re-examined and, according to the North Carolina version, Captain Terrell's friends finally demonstrated to him that he had been mistaken in his report. Thereupon he, being "a gallant officer and a true gentleman," agreed to withdraw the language offensive to the North Carolinians. The sensible settlement was communicated to the seconds of Belo and Cussons just in time for them to intervene. The principals were already on the line awaiting the signal for the third fire. The Alabama version was that Connally's second withdrew the challenge. In any event, both sides amply demonstrated their feelings and the personal recklessness rampant in the Southern army.

The Fifty-fifth claimed that in discipline and experience it was one of the finest Southern regiments. The men took a great pride in Connally as tactician and disciplinarian. In one respect, at least, the regiment probably did excel. Where some of the regiments had mere fife and drum corps, the Fifty-fifth had a band of seventeen pieces. The men had good gray uniforms, and each company was recruited to full strength. Said the adjutant, "No regiment . . . ever had better field officers. They were all . . . erect, soldierly in their bearing, proud of their regiment and enthusiastic in their patriotism." Fresh, disciplined, eager, the Fifty-fifth North Carolina made a noteworthy addition to Lee's army, and gave it distinguished service at Gettysburg.

Chapter X

SHATTERED HOPES AT GETTYSBURG

To RETURN MOMENTARILY to the beginning of Lee's Pennsylvania campaign, it should be noted that North Carolina units of Brigadier General Stephen Dodson Ramseur's brigade led the invasion. This brigade was the first to cross the Potomac.

Quite appropriately the first command to touch the Maryland shore was Governor Vance's old company, the "Rough and Ready Guards," of Asheville, a part of Colonel Risden T. Bennett's Fourteenth North Carolina Infantry, which marched into Hagerstown, Maryland, and thence to Carlisle, Pennsylvania.

Ramseur's brigade played a key role in the battle of July 1. By a skillful flanking movement the brigade rolled up the right of the Federal line west of the town and drove it through the streets to the protection of Cemetery Ridge. When the Federal army, retiring precipitously, came straggling back through Gettysburg in the late afternoon, Ramseur's four North Carolina regiments — the Second, Fourth, Fourteenth and Thirtieth—thundered into the town from the northwest at almost the same instant Perrin's South Carolinians, of Pender's division, entered from the west.

Intrepid Major General William Dorsey Pender, the highest ranking North Carolina soldier on the field, whose division had just dislodged the First Corps of the Federal army at the Seminary and cleared Seminary Ridge, rode ahead of his men and witnessed their advance into the town. His division — the "Light Division" which had won glory under A. P. Hill — included the North Carolina brigades of James H. Lane and Alfred M. Scales, as well as Perrin's South Carolinians and Edward L. Thomas' Georgians. Scales sustained heavy losses in his assault on the Seminary and he himself was wounded.

Ineffectual and costly among the attacks on the first day of the battle was that of Alfred Iverson's North Carolina brigade of Rode's division, which Iverson hurled against the two Federal brigades of Baxter and Paul, concealed behind a stone wall of the Forney farm northwest of Gettysburg. The brigade was pinned down in an open field under a storm of fire from front and flanks, but fought gallantly until relieved by Ramseur. General Robert E. Rodes, riding over the field after the Federal army had been pressed back, found Iverson's dead lying in rows in a "distinctly marked line of battle." They were collected and buried in common graves behind the lines, which became known as "Iverson's Pits."

Daniel's brigade, composed of the Thirty-second, Forty-third, Forty-fifth and Fifty-third North Carolina Regiments and the Second North Carolina Battalion, suffered its heavy casualties in two grueling assaults, the first against Stone's Pennsylvania "Bucktail" brigade at the McPherson farm on the Cashtown Road and at the nearby railroad cut. Here the deadly battle swayed back and forth during the afternoon of July 1 until the Bucktails, sadly reduced by their gallant defense, were pushed toward Gettysburg, where Ramseur took up the pursuit.

In the later phase of the battle on Culp's Hill, Daniel's brigade was lent to Ewell's corps and with it fought in the deadly, stubborn fray on the morning of July 3 in which the Confederate attack was at length repulsed. On Culp's Hill other North Carolina regiments won distinction. In the attack by Steuart's brigade of Edward Johnson's division on the night of July 2, the First and Third North Carolina Regiments charged up the heights. After desperate fighting in the darkness, elements of the First North Carolina and the First Maryland carried a section of the Federal intrenchments. The Carolina storming party was led by Lieutenant Green Martin of Company B, who fell mortally wounded at the moment of triumph. Had this success come in daylight so that it might have been exploited, Edward Johnson very likely could have captured the Baltimore turnpike, cut this lifeline of the Federal army and forced Meade to evacuate Culp's and Cemetery Hills. But the Federal Twelfth Corps, heavily reinforced by other of Meade's units, was present before daylight on the morning of July 3, and the trenches it had lost on the previous evening were wrested from Steuart's Confederates.

Still more menacing to Meade's army was the assault at sundown

Major General
William Dorsey Pender

on July 2 on East Cemetery Hill, launched by Hoke's North Carolina brigade, commanded by Colonel Isaac E. Avery while Hoke was recovering from the severe wound he had received in the Chancellorsville campaign. Avery co-operated in the attack with Harry T. Hays' brigade of "Louisiana Tigers." These two brigades stormed up the hill, drove off the Federals who manned the stone wall along the heights, and captured the Federal batteries.

But here as elsewhere in this desperately fought battle that was so lacking in concert between the various attacking groups, the two small brigades were unsupported. They commanded for a moment the very heart of the Federal position, but their strength was wasted away in the inferno which lighted the hill with flashes of flame. Fresh troops thrown in by the vigilant Federal General Winfield S. Hancock charged through the darkness and forced the Carolinians and "Tigers" back to the base of the hill.

Colonel Avery was mortally wounded in this attack. While his men were pressing past him where he fell, he had time to write a note to Lieutenant Colonel Samuel McDowell Tate, who succeeded him as commander of the Sixth North Carolina Regiment. The note will be remembered long in the story of North Carolina at Gettysburg. Avery's brief message was, "Tell my father I fell with my face to the enemy." It was written with a lead pencil, though one of the stories frequently told about it was that the Colonel wrote it with his own blood.

Probably the most critical loss of the battle was that of North Carolina's Major General W. Dorsey Pender, who fell as he was preparing to take his division into action on the late afternoon of July 2. He died at Staunton, Virginia, on the journey home at the age of twenty-nine. General Lee, in one of his few discussions of the battle, disclosed the significance he attached to Pender's fall. "I shall ever believe," he said, "if General Pender had remained on his horse half an hour longer we would have carried the enemy's position." Major Joseph A. Englehard, Pender's adjutant general, gave this similar opinion that, "Seldom has the service suffered more in the loss of one man."

On the third day at Gettysburg Lee directed his most determined assault against the Federal center on Cemetery Ridge. He placed his assaulting column of about 14,000 troops under Longstreet's command. The force included Pickett's fresh Virginia division, which had been guarding the rear at Chambersburg during the first two days of

the fighting: Heth's division, now commanded by Pettigrew, composed of North Carolina, Alabama, Mississippi and Tennessee troops; and Trimble's demi-division, composed of the two North Carolina brigades of Lane and Scales. The Carolinians advanced to the left of Pickett, while on his right were Wilcox's Alabama and Lang's Florida brigades. Scales had been wounded and his brigade was commanded by Colonel W. L. J. Lowrance of the Thirty-fourth North Carolina.

The attack, made across a mile of open ground, seemed almost foredoomed to failure; still, the resolute troops pressed on through a devastating artillery fire from Little Round Top and Cemetery Ridge and stormed up to the Federal lines protected by a low stone wall near the crest of the ridge. But the odds were too severe. The repulse was bloody and costly in killed, wounded and captured. The brigade of Pickett's division which penetrated the first Federal line was commanded by Brigadier General Lewis A. Armistead, a native of New Bern, North Carolina, who fell mortally wounded at the head of his men. He led his brigade on foot, carried his hat on his sword point, and called on his soldiers to follow him over the wall.

The claim is well founded that the farthest advance made in the Pickett-Pettigrew-Trimble assault was that of the Fifty-fifth North Carolina of Davis' brigade, Pettigrew's division. There is abundant testimony also that North Carolina units carried on the attack until the futility of further loss became apparent, and were the last beaten back across the Emmitsburg Road, though the story of their conduct was distorted in a lengthy account of the assault sent immediately after the battle to a Richmond newspaper. This account, which termed Pettigrew's men "raw troops," charged that they broke and exposed Pickett's division, which in consequence of this defection was forced back. The newspaper version unfortunately was followed in almost the exact language in some of the early histories of the battle. A storm of complaint arose in North Carolina, and the facts were gathered. Testimony by many participants and a correction of the record by research have caused the version to be accepted in careful accounts of the battle that North Carolian troops performed nobly on all parts of that field and made the farthest advance in this final, desperate assault.

North Carolina lost 770 of her soldiers on the field at Gettysburg, a loss greater than that of any other state. The second heaviest death toll at Gettysburg was Georgia's with 435 killed; then Virginia, 399;

Mississippi, 258; South Carolina, 217; Alabama, 204; and other Southern states in lesser numbers. Of course the states farther south did not have as many units on the field and consequently suffered lighter casualties. One-fourth of the total casualties, killed and wounded, were among North Carolina troops. Captain S. A. Ashe, the distinguished North Carolina historian and writer about the Civil War, who served as assistant adjutant general under Pender, made a detailed study of what he termed the "Pettigrew-Pickett Charge" and concluded that while North Carolina brigades did not lose as many prisoners, they "suffered greater losses, advanced the farthest, and remained the longest."

Some North Carolinians fought in important commands on the Union side at Gettysburg. Brigadier General Solomon P. Meredith, a Quaker who had moved in early manhood from Guilford County, North Carolina, to Cambridge City, Indiana, commanded one of the most celebrated Federal units, the "Iron Brigade" which opposed Pettigrew's determined assault. Meredith was wounded severely on the first day of the battle.

Another incident involving North Carolina officers showed the confusion of loyalties that were a part of this war. When Daniel's North Carolina brigade stood at last triumphant at the Seminary on the first day of the battle, Colonel Thomas S. Kenan, of the Forty-third North Carolina, had time to inspect the condition of his men. While thus engaged, one of his lieutenants, Henry E. Shepherd, reported that the lieutenant colonel of the Seventh Wisconsin Regiment was lying grievously wounded nearby and was a North Carolinian. Lieutenant Shepherd was concerned because both he and the wounded Federal were from Fayetteville.

Kenan went out with a detail, found Lieutenant Colonel John B. Callis, of Lancaster, Wisconsin, just beyond the ridge, and had him carried into the Seminary where Southern surgeons were caring for the wounded.

"You are my prisoner and I will treat you well," said the Confederate. "I may be yours later on."

Callis, the Federal, presented his spurs to Kenan. He said he had left North Carolina with his father when he was ten and had moved to Wisconsin Territory. His father had remonstrated when he joined the Federal army, saying that he would be fighting his own flesh and blood, but the younger man's sentiments were with his adopted people.

Here again high officers who opposed each other, as was the case with Pettigrew and Meredith, and Burgwyn and Morrow, had been born a relatively short distance apart in the South.

The Pennsylvania campaign ended on a sad note. General Pettigrew commanded Lee's rear guard at the crossing of the Potomac on the retreat to Virginia. In an attack by a Federal cavalry patrol at Falling Waters he was mortally wounded. He died near Bunker Hill, Virginia, mourned as one of the great soldiers North Carolina gave to the Confederate cause.

ZEB VANCE – DYNAMO OF THE CONFEDERACY

Meantime, under the stimulus of war, North Carolina was experiencing at home something of an industrial and commercial revolution. A society that had been almost wholly agricultural, heavily engaged in the production of cotton, tobacco, tar products and grains, where it was tacitly understood that much of the upland corn crop would be marketed in bottles or stored for home use in demijohns, suddenly found itself whipped into a provisioner of the Southern armies.

As Virginia was overrun by the Federals and the rich Shenandoah Valley and the fertile Potomac and Rappahannock River counties were taken out of production for the South, the call on North Carolina became increasingly urgent. Governor Vance, ardently imbued with the spirit of victory, was prepared to give wholehearted response to the Confederacy's great need of food, clothing and equipment.

While the young men of the State were battling on the firing line, the bulk of the home public under the spur of the zealous Vance went to work in shirt sleeves to give devoted service to the Southern cause. At the beginning of the war the State had few manufacturers, being dependent on the North and Great Britain even for such homely objects as broom handles and water buckets — items which the Governor himself referred to by way of illustration — or such essentials as farm tools and machinery down to scissors and kitchen knives. Cotton had been moving north before the war and North Carolina had become a heavy grower, but it manufactured less than half its consumption of cotton goods. It manufactured less than a tenth of its needs of woolens or shoes, and not one-twentieth of its iron requirements. As far as was possible Vance corrected all this. He stimulated textile manufacturing and soon was buying virtually the full output of thirty-nine cotton mills and eight woolen mills in the State. Thus the North Carolina textile industry came into its first bloom. In Raleigh he established a factory that made soldiers' uniforms and overcoats, while everywhere the women were busy with their sewing. His agents combed the country for wool and leather.

Where he could, he took over obligations which normally would have fallen to the central Confederate government at Richmond. One of the results of the home enterprise was that North Carolina troops were in most instances well-uniformed. There was little warrant for the term "Lee's ragged veterans" where North Carolina soldiers were concerned. Governor Vance was too good a provider. As the war moved on, the quality of the uniforms improved. Vance relieved the Richmond government of the necessity of clothing North Carolina soldiers. Until the State was overrun by invading armies and the manufacturing plants were captured or destroyed, he kept the home front busy on uniforms, though the clothing manufacturing facilities were unable to remain ahead or abreast of the supplies of uniform cloth he accumulated. At the end of the war he had large quantities of bolted materials on hand.

He marshaled public sentiment and restricted the acreage of cotton and tobacco, giving preference to food. He stopped all legal and even most illegal distilling, much to the anguish of some old-time farmers who wrote to him plaintively about the heavy infestation of snakes. Lee's army was fed mainly from the alluvial lowlands of the eastern counties. Said Vance: "The fields everywhere were green and golden with corn and wheat. . . . Old men and women . . . guided the plow and children followed with the hoe in the gaping furrows."

The Governor sent agents to the Clyde River in Scotland where they bought a ship, the *Lord Clyde.* They rechristened her the *Ad-Vance,* or *Advance,* and disproved the old superstition that it is unlucky to change a ship's name. She made eleven trips from Wilmington to Nassau, Bermuda, or Halifax. Whether or not she was named after the Governor is a disputed point of little consequence, but she should have been. The Governor apparently thought so, for he referred to her as the *Ad-Vance,* and not as some have insisted, the *Advance.*

She must have saved a large number of North Carolina lives with the medical supplies she was able to slip past the blockaders vigilantly plying off Cape Hatteras, Cape Lookout, and Cape Fear. Her first entry was the signal for an ovation. The people of Wilmington greeted her with ecstacy when she appeared with her bulging cargo, mainly cloth. This was put aboard a special, guarded train, transported to Raleigh and turned over at once to the women of the city, who with their needles soon had it sewed by hand into gleaming new uniforms.

Other steamers were quickly plying back and forth between Wilmington and the supply centers of the Bahamas, where North Carolina cotton might be exchanged for the commodities urgently needed both by the army and home public. It happened that as long as Fort Fisher, which protected Wilmington, held out against Northern attacks the Confederacy survived, and when the fort fell the Confederacy passed. Some have counted these events as inseparable and therefore have regarded the loss of Fort Fisher in early 1865 as the decisive battle of the war. More accurately, it merely marked another and well-nigh the final step down the ladder toward the inevitable end.

The *Ad-Vance* brought in enough gray woolen cloth for 250,000 uniforms and 12,000 overcoats, plus 250,000 pairs of shoes and 50,000 blankets, along with bacon, coffee, and the imperatively required medicines. Vance encouraged or established munitions factories for powder, cartridges and firearms. The State was raked clean of metal. The churches offered their bells for the cannon that sounded across the Virginia and Pennsylvania hills.

Vance not only fitted out North Carolina soldiers but turned over large quantities of clothing, blankets and shoes for troops from other states. At one time he sent 14,000 complete suits of clothing to Longstreet's corps, which included no North Carolina units.

The industrious Governor was able at a critical moment in the spring of 1863 to send up a large quantity of bacon to the Confederate commissary, which forwarded it immediately to Lee's poorly rationed army. It helped to build energy before the step-off for Pennsylvania, where the heavily loaded granaries and herds of beef requisitioned and paid for by Lee's quartermasters relieved the pressure on North Carolina for much of the summer. All through the war he provided wheat, bacon and fodder to Confederate armies.

While the gifted, learned, but pedantic Jefferson Davis mulled over imponderables, Vance was a dynamo surcharging the Confederacy with action. Davis might concern himself with abstractions but Vance dealt in cattle, hogs and corn. This man of tireless energy gave incalculable aid to the South and in doing so came to be deeply admired by the majority of the people of his State, whose interests he always jealously guarded against the central government at Richmond, as well as against the Northern invaders. A factor which endeared him to the ordinary citizen was his solid integrity. A rugged man, he epitomized the strength of his native Blue Ridge mountains. Someone has associated with his personality the words "droll, imperturbable, quizzical and leonine." To these it might be added that he was one of the best storytellers of his time, though his biographers will have difficulty putting some of his men's-room witticisms into print.

How Zeb Vance during his speaking tour in Virginia electrified Lee's army was described by Colonel Joseph Caldwell Webb of the Twenty-seventh North Carolina Infantry which at that time, just before the Wilderness campaign, was in the brigade of Joseph R. Davis of Harry Heth's division.

Colonel Webb's letters were brought to light in 1962 by Thomas Felix Hickerson, Kenan Professor Emeritus of the University of North Carolina, in his collection of old papers and diaries published under the title of *Echoes of Happy Valley*.

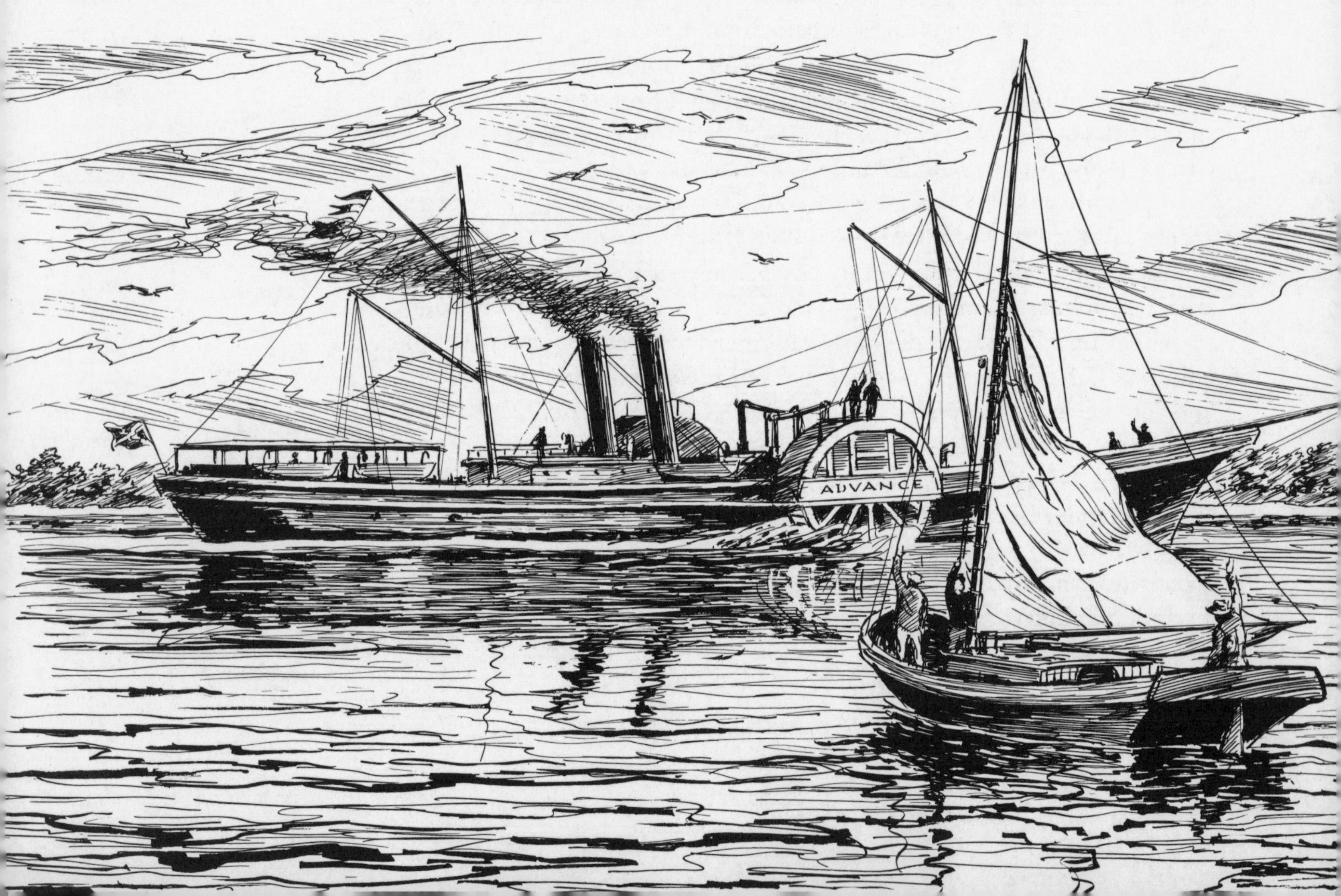

Writing on April 4, 1864, to his aunt Robina Norwood, a resident of Hillsboro, North Carolina, Colonel Webb gave a glimpse of one of Vance's meetings he attended. He had returned from leave and found the army "all ablaze with excitement." Vance has been speaking through Ewell's and A. P. Hill's corps, Longstreet's being absent.

Vance was scheduled to review the brigade of Davis and Brigadier General William W. Kirkland, of Hillsboro, on Tuesday, April 5. A downpour of rain turned the reviewing field into a quagmire, but on the next day Vance spoke to about 6,000 men, many being from states other than North Carolina, "who seem to vie with our own soldiers in admiration of him."

"General Stewart [*sic*] has been with him nearly all the time since he came, and a number of other generals have been to hear him every time he spoke. Gen'l Lee has heard him twice, and I understand that old Gen'l Ewell has nearly shaken his wooden leg to pieces laughing at his jokes. I don't think I ever saw a more attentive or enthusiastic audience than he had here, notwithstanding the men had to stand in mud and water all the time he was speaking. . . ."

All the while Governor Vance had to contend with invasions by Federal armies along the North Carolina seacoast which would have appalled and vanquished lesser souls. His constant problem was lack of soldiers on the home front, since most of the men from the Old North State were fighting in Virginia. (An illustrated account of the war along the North Carolina coast has been published by the State Department of Archives and History under the title of *North Carolina as a Civil War Battleground, 1861-1865,* and is available from the Department, Box 1881, Raleigh, North Carolina. These campaigns consequently will not be dealt with in detail here.)

The object of the invading armies was to move inland from the North Carolina shore, sever the railroad connection leading south from Richmond and isolate Lee's army and Virginia from the rest of the Confederacy. Possessing control of the sea, the Federal government could land and supply its forces at almost any point of its choosing, but as the invading armies worked inland they encountered the strong and for four years the successful resistance of Southern forces, mostly North Carolinians under North Carolina generals.

The principal North Carolina campaigns, in summary, were the successful descent by the Federal General Benjamin F. Butler and a strong naval force on Hatteras Inlet and the Outer Banks, protected by Forts Hatteras and Clark, in late August, 1861; the capture of Roanoke Island and New Bern by the combined land and naval operation of the Federal General Ambrose E. Burnside; the operations against eastern North Carolina towns by the Federal General John G. Foster; D. H. Hill's abortive siege of the Federal forces in Washington, North Carolina, and in the next year the unsuccessful effort to recapture New Bern; General Robert F. Hoke's brilliant recapture of Plymouth and of devastated Washington in 1864; the series of operations against Fort Fisher at the mouth of the Cape Fear River; sporadic fighting in the western North Carolina mountains; and finally, the invasion of the State by General William Tecumseh Sherman's army that had just gutted Georgia and South Carolina, and the last ditch "Battle of the Generals" at Bentonville, the closing major engagement of the war.

North Carolina was the last of the Confederate states to be overrun, though the vastness of Texas made subjugation next to impossible. At the end of the war Northern armies crashed in from the east, south and west, and substantially all important points in North Carolina were garrisoned by blue-clad soldiers.

Chapter

WILDERNESS, SPOTSYLVANIA AND CHICKAMAUGA

Before the dramatic closing days of the Confederacy, twenty-one months of bitter fighting were to follow Lee's retreat from Pennsylvania.

What some of the Federal commanders had tried to accomplish by strategy and maneuver, the new commander in chief of the Union forces, Major General Ulysses S. Grant, undertook with heavy columns and brute force.

Through the Wilderness, where "Old Joe Hooker" had fought Chancellorsville against Lee, the heavy battle now reverberated day after day as Grant sought vainly to break and destroy Lee's army in the thickets. Though his numbers vastly exceeded Lee's, he was at length forced to give up his frontal assault and attempt to march around Lee's flank to Spotsylvania. But Lee was not to be cut off from Richmond. Anticipating Grant's move, he was in force at Spotsylvania when the Federal army camped in front of the town. Grant settled down with the declaration that he would "fight it out on this line if it takes all summer."

Here occurred one of the unfortunate losses of the war to the Confederate cause, the capture of Edward Johnson's division, formerly Stonewall Jackson's, by the Second Corps of the Federal army commanded by Major General Hancock. Drawing up his four divisions in a formidable mass, Hancock attacked at dawn and crashed through the salient of Lee's Spotsylvania lines known as the "Mule Shoe," which had been stripped of artillery because of Lee's anticipated march that morning. The Confederate salient was overrun, and the defenders, taken in the rear, were scooped up and made prisoners. Lee's entire army was placed in extreme jeopardy.

At the moment of crisis a single North Carolina brigade set up a defense against the onrushing Federals and held long enough for Lee to arrange and man a new line. This was Brigadier General Robert D. Johnston's brigade, composed of the Fifth, Twelfth, Twentieth and Twenty-third North Carolina Regiments — the brigade which under Iverson had been caught and cut to pieces before the stone wall of the Forney farm at Gettysburg. Now, with fresh recruits to fill some of the gaps and being better led than on the Pennsylvania invasion, the brigade made a stanch stand and cleaned the record of its earlier, bitter defeat.

General Robert D. Johnston, a native of Lincoln County and graduate of the University of North Carolina, had begun the war as a captain of Company K, Twenty-third North Carolina. He was advanced due to conspicuous service on the Peninsula and in the Maryland and Pennsylvania campaigns until he became a brigadier general when only twenty-four years old.

One of his regiments, the Twentieth North Carolina, had engaged in a sentimental instead of a leaden exchange with the Northern army when they were facing each other sixteen months earlier across the Rapidan River at Fredericksburg. The Twentieth had a good band which liked to serenade with the old songs, but including the sprightly new battle air "Dixie." A Northern band across the river played the tune back as a friendly greeting. Then the North Carolina musicians favored the Northerners with "Yankee Doodle." Seemingly by prearrangement, both bands suddenly struck up the most treasured song of all, "Home, Sweet Home," and there were plenty of tears as the refrain rolled down the river swelling from the voices of thousands of soldiers of both armies.

While Johnston was holding, John B. Gordon was rushing his brigade from the rear to help seal the breach that had been opened and through which the entire Union army seemed likely to pour. This was one of the occasions when General Lee, aware of the desperate situation that confronted his army, mounted Traveler and made ready to lead personally the Confederate counterattack. But he found his men unwilling to go forward until he went to a place of greater safety. This well-known "General Lee to the rear" incident showed the deep affection of the men for their commander. All day they battled, and by nightfall the deadly Federal thrust had been repelled.

North Carolina brigades suffered heavy losses in the hard fought battles of the Wilderness and at Spotsylvania. Substantially all of the First and Third North Carolina Regiments, of Steuart's brigade, Edward Johnson's division, were taken prisoners in Hancock's break-through. Colonel H. A. Brown, commanding the First North Carolina, was captured, liberated and recaptured three times in the confusion of the foggy morning.

North Carolina troops were active also in repulsing Grant's bloody and foolhardy assault on the Confederate trenches at Cold Harbor, where the Union army lost 12,000 men, about 9,000 in the appallingly short period of eight minutes. The corps of Hancock, Baldy Smith and Wright were caught in a cross fire in front of Lee's formidable defenses, in what the Confederate General E. McIver Law described as "not war, but murder." The assault showed Grant that he could not break through the front door into Richmond and sent him south of the James River for the long siege of Petersburg.

Meantime the war was moving in the western theater toward the battles of Atlanta and Nashville and Sherman's march across Georgia. No North Carolina units were engaged with Pemberton's army in the

defense and surrender of Vicksburg, although the Twenty-ninth, Thirty-ninth and Sixtieth North Carolina Regiments were with Joseph E. Johnston in Mississippi, where he undertook unsuccessfully to give Pemberton relief. The Twenty-ninth and Sixtieth had been earlier with Bragg's army in Tennessee. The Twenty-ninth fought under Colonel Robert B. Vance, brother of the Governor, at Murfreesboro, or Stone's River, in the stubborn two-day battle that had one of the highest casualty rates per numbers engaged of the war. Vance took command of the brigade when Brigadier General James E. Rains was killed by a minié ball.

At Chickamauga, the great battle of the western armies fought on September 19 and 20, 1863, North Carolina regiments had key roles. The Sixtieth made the farthest advance in General Breckinridge's assault on the Federal left flank, which threatened to cut off the Federals from their base in Chattanooga. The Thirty-ninth was a part of McNair's "Star Brigade of Chickamauga," which was in General Bushrod R. Johnson's division of Longstreet's corps. This division cut through the center of the Federal army, which was commanded by the able strategist William S. Rosecrans. Longstreet drove the Federal right wing back into Chattanooga. Colonel David Coleman of the Thirty-ninth took command of the "Star Brigade" when General McNair was wounded.

The Fifty-eighth North Carolina, with the rest of Kelly's brigade, advanced alongside Gracie's Alabama brigade and Trigg's Florida brigade, all of Preston's division, against the Federal General George H. Thomas' position on Snodgrass Hill, in Longstreet's last desperate effort to drive the left wing of the Union army after the right wing into Chattanooga. Thomas resolutely beat off the attacks until darkness, earned the sobriquet of the "Rock of Chickamauga," then retired to Rossville and Chattanooga.

Some writers have contended that the Fifty-eighth Regiment made in Preston's advance the farthest penetration of the Federal lines — a claim difficult to sustain in such a fluid battle. Certainly it was Trigg's brigade which reached the Federal rear and brought about the capture of the last three Federal regiments left on Snodgrass Hill. In the pursuit of the Federal army toward Chattanooga, Forrest's cavalry led the way. The claim lacks the definiteness and supporting evidence of that of the Fifty-fifth North Carolina at Gettysburg.

BENTONVILLE–
BATTLE OF DESPERATION

Bentonville, the last major engagement of the Confederacy and the largest battle ever fought on North Carolina soil, was unlike any other battle in this war, and different in some respects from any other in the long course of history. Never were so many ardent soldiers willing to bank themselves into a forlorn hope and sacrifice their lives so freely in a last desperate effort for a cause that already was obviously lost. And perhaps in no operation since the Children's Crusade were so many fledgling youths — the last crop of boys from North Carolina towns and farms — aligned in the marching ranks.

At Bentonville they stood and fought with resolution and hope, but fought vainly against the hardened veterans Sherman had brought up from Vicksburg, Chattanooga and Kenesaw Mountain. Due to the presence of this North Carolina junior brigade and to the devotion of the seasoned soldiers who knew in their hearts that the war already was lost, Bentonville, this sunset battle of the prostrate South, was one of the inspiring episodes of American history.

Little has been written about Bentonville in the popular accounts. It can be described here only in bare outline. Sherman was rolling up with his army from Atlanta and Savannah, Georgia, with a 400-mile trail of blackened country behind him and the ruins of Columbia, South Carolina, the "nest of secession," still stark and smoking in his wake. His great army of 60,000 men, marching jauntily ahead with the high confidence won by repeated triumphs over scant bands of defenders, entered North Carolina and on March 11, 1865, captured with ease the old Federal arsenal city of Fayetteville.

As though the vast army Sherman already commanded was not sufficient to reduce North Carolina, the Federal government made plans to reinforce it, first with a column under Major General Alfred H. Terry, the captor of Fort Fisher, coming up from Wilmington, and by another corps under Major General John M. Schofield which had been transported by water to New Bern and was moving northwest to Goldsboro. General Braxton Bragg with a small Confederate force was fighting and retiring in front of Schofield. Then Grant at this stage intended to send Sheridan down from the Shenandoah Valley so that he and Sherman, the two "total war" generals of the North, might have a fling together at North Carolina's unspoiled resources.

While Sherman was near Fayetteville he wrote one night to Terry about the expected coming of Sheridan, saying the cavalryman could have a present of every horse in North Carolina with which to play at what he termed "the grand and beautiful game of war." War was indeed a "beautiful game" to the conqueror. Not in all his moods did Sherman judge that "war is hell!" Waxing enthusiastic, he employed in his letter to Terry the phrase already applied to Georgia: "I'll make all North Carolina howl." Sherman was exultant in those days, mopping up the South and gaining the plaudits of the Northern press while the more lethargic Grant was still stalled in front of the Petersburg trenches.

At Fayetteville Sherman destroyed machine shops, foundries and the arsenal and handled the torch freely around some public buildings but did not sack the town. Here he received visible evidence that Terry was at last in the coveted port of the blockade-runners, Wilmington. The Federal army tug *Davison* steamed up the Cape Fear River with news that both Terry and Schofield were in good shape and moving toward the proposed concentration.

The jucture at Goldsboro of Sherman's "bummers" from Georgia with the armies of Terry and Schofield coming in from the coast would give Sherman a force of about 90,000, even without Sheridan, whom Grant decided to hold in Virginia. Against this power General Joseph E. Johnston might array less than 30,000 illy-equipped men.

There is something more formidable than numbers in the momentum of an army on an unchecked invasion. Like the acceleration of an avalanche plunging down the mountainside, Sherman was collecting impetus as he moved through the heart of the Carolinas. The peach orchards were in their full beauty and the lilacs in fragrance as he swung gaily out of Fayetteville toward the trysting place with Terry and Schofield. His army marched in two columns, the right wing com-

General Braxton Bragg

manded by Major General Oliver O. Howard and the left by Major General Henry W. Slocum.

Slocum was an upstate New Yorker who had been graduated seventh in his class at West Point. While serving in the old army in South Carolina he had studied law under Judge B. C. Presley, an eminent member of the Charleston bar. Against the South he had fought carefully and effectively, but never sensationally, in numerous major battles, beginning with First Manassas and extending through Gettysburg, Chattanooga and Atlanta. Now he was about to serve as field commander of Federal forces in the largest of North Carolina battles. One of Slocum's contributions was to leave for posterity the most exact and minute details produced during the war on how to destroy a railroad. That had become something of a science in Sherman's army but Slocum's studied methods capped them all. A hard fighter, he was among the first after the war to forget it, hold out a magnanimous hand to the South, and let bygones be bygones.

Sherman was not seeking combat until after he had effected his consolidation at Goldsboro. But at Averasboro, thirty miles north of Fayetteville, he encountered a delaying force which Hardee had brought up from Charleston, accompanied by a South Carolina artillery regiment commanded by Charlestonian Alfred Rhett. Hardee fought stubbornly from noon until nightfall and all through the next day. Rhett was captured, and eventually Sherman encircled and dislodged the Confederates, who left behind 108 dead and 68 wounded. The Federal loss was 77 killed and 477 wounded. A greater battle by far was this than Bethel; yet it rarely gets a line in the history books.

After Averasboro Sherman was alert, but that he did not anticipate a formidable attack might be seen from the fact that he was traveling with Howard's right wing nearest the approaching elements of Terry and Schofield, instead of with Slocum's left wing, the western and more exposed flank of the army as it moved north. But on this left wing Johnston had been bringing together the best kind of an army he could collect in that late afternoon of Confederate power, and on March 19, 1865, at Bentonville, he struck Slocum with sudden and arresting force.

What followed has sometimes been called the "battle of the generals" because behind Johnston were aligned few soldiers but a galaxy of Confederate great. Never had so many four-star generals, lieutenant generals and major generals appeared on a single field. "Beau Sabreur" Pierre G. T. Beauregard was second in command. Bragg, another full general, commanded a corps. Lieutenant Generals Joseph Wheeler and Wade Hampton led gaunt specters of their once glorious cavalry commands. Lieutenant Generals William J. Hardee and Stephen D. Lee, great tacticians of the western armies, led depleted corps that looked more like earlier brigades.

What remained of Bragg's great Army of Tennessee, which at Chickamauga had won an outstanding Conferedate victory and driven Rosecrans pell mell from the field, was compressed into a scant corps at Bentonville. It was commanded by Lieutenant General Alexander P. Stewart, known affectionately to his men as "Old Straight," a great educator and able general admired in both armies. Other major generals in active command were Robert F. Hoke, great on any field; Lafayette McLaws, who had broken the Peach Orchard line at Gettysburg; Benjamin F. Cheatham, hard fighter at Shiloh, Murfreesboro and Chickamauga; D. H. Hill, who had held the rank of lieutenant general temporarily during the Chickamauga campaign; William W. Loring, known as "Old Blizzards," who had lost an arm in Mexico and shown his courage by clashing not only often with the Federals, but with Stonewall Jackson as well; Edward C. Walthall, a lawyer who had risen from first lieutanant of the Yalobusha Rifles to eminence in the West; John Calvin Brown, who had distinguished

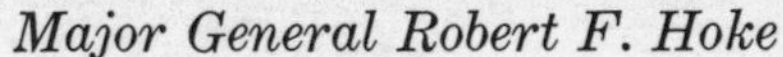

Major General Robert F. Hoke

Major General D. H. Hill

himself at Chickamauga and succeeded to the command of the lamented Pat Cleburne's division after the battle of Franklin; Patton Anderson, the Mississippi physician who had stamped himself as a gifted combat leader on nearly every field where he served; Carter L. Stevenson, who had commanded a hard luck division under the unfortunate Pemberton at Vicksburg and Bragg on Missionary Ridge; Matthew C. Butler, the South Carolina cavalryman who would serve as a major general also in the war with Spain; and another cavalryman, Pierce Manning Butler Young. Beneath this talent there were brigadier generals too numerous to mention in this account. All of these high ranking officers commanded detachments of some sort in an army having approximately 17,000 infantry soldiers, eight batteries of field artillery and 5,000 cavalry, an aggregate of about 22,000 soldiers. Three full generals, five lieutenant generals, and eleven major generals were on the field. Of the twenty-two brigadier generals, seventeen held infantry and five, cavalry commands. Truly it was a "battle of the generals!"

But there was standing room and advancing room for the privates. The action was launched from a wooded hill overlooking a cleared field that had been selected by Lieutenant General Wade Hampton as suitable for the Southern attack. Johnston confirmed the position when he brought his fragments together at Bentonville village. The Southern army had reached the position by a night march, and Johnston had directed the construction of earthworks while Hampton's cavalry retarded the progress of the advancing Federals to a slow march with frequent halts. Then the forward division of Sherman's left wing, Brigadier General William P. Carlin's First Division of the famous Federal Fourteenth Army Corps, came up against the Southern infantry. The Fourteenth Corps was commanded by Brigadier General Jefferson C. Davis, who on his earlier visit to the Carolinas had been a second lieutenant inside Fort Sumter when it capitulated to Beauregard. Though there had been substitutions of units and many replacements, this Federal Fourteenth Corps was once the grand fighting body that had been organized and trained by General George H. Thomas, and under him had held the center at Murfreesboro and a little later had given him fame as the "Rock of Chickamauga."

Carlin was rudely hauled up by the fire from Bragg's corps, but

Johnston could not assail the advancing Federals until Hardee brought up one of his main elements and filled in the gap between Bragg and Stewart, which meantime was held merely by Hampton's batteries. When Hardee arrived he was directed by Johnston at the request of Bragg to send a division to the support of Hoke, though that General repulsed the enemy so vigorously that the aid was not needed. This was the initial phase of the battle, the repulse of Carlin's division by Hoke.

Then came the spirited Confederate attack of 17,000 infantry and 5,000 bobtailed cavalry against Slocum's 30,000, supported by Howard's 30,000 marching on a parallel road. The March afternoon was wearing on when between 3:15 and 3:30 o'clock Hardee moved forward in conjunction with Stewart, routed Carlin's division and drove a section of the Fourteenth Corps back at a run on the Federal Twentieth Corps, commanded by Brigadier General Alpheus S. Williams. This was the second phase, an emphatic Confederate triumph. But the Twentieth held and the Confederate attack was arrested.

Meantime Sherman, hearing the heavy firing and learning that Slocum's left had been pounced on by a Confederate army he estimated as 40,000 strong, spurred the Fifteenth and Seventeenth Corps of Howard's wing toward Bentonville, which would bring a concentration of the entire force Sherman had marched up from Columbia, and enough weight to crush Johnston's game but meager army underfoot. Johnston must have known the odds were desperate, but at that late season where were better odds to be obtained?

Little fighting occurred on the next day, Monday, March 20. Sherman, strangely indisposed to fight to the finish until he had effected his consolidation at Goldsboro, did not press the engagement, even when, on March 21, the Seventeenth Corps, coming on the field from Howard's right wing, took Johnston in flank. Major General Joseph A. Mower, commanding the First Division of that corps, understood that his purpose was to fight; and when the combat was renewed on March 21, he struck with unexpected fury the extreme left of the Confederate line, outflanking McLaws' trenches and plunging through the cavalry skirmishers and patrols. Mower, bold and combative, led his men on foot and approached within 200 yards of Johnston's headquarters and the bridge where the Bentonville road crossed Mill Creek. The significance of this bridge was that it controlled Johnston's route of withdrawal. Had Mower captured it and been reinforced by

Sherman's ample reserves, the entire Confederate army might easily have been bagged.

Why he did not is disputed. Sherman's biographer, Lloyd Lewis, says Sherman halted the advance voluntarily and by doing so lost his last opportunity to be rated a great combat commander. Sherman in his *Memoirs* said he ordered Mower to desist. The Southern view, taken from the accounts of those on the field, is that Mower was attacked by some of Hampton's troopers, by Henderson's Georgia brigade reduced to about 200 infantrymen, and by the Eighth Texas and Fourth Tennessee Cavalry Regiments of Wheeler's command. Far from withdrawing voluntarily, the retirement, as described by a lieutenant of the Fifty-first North Carolina, was disorderly: "The rout of the enemy was complete and they were soon driven back beyond our lines. As they retreated in confusion the slaughter was terrible." General Hardee arrived to lead this counterattack. Wade Hampton said it was "so sudden and so impetuous that it carried everything before it." If, as Sherman said, Mower was ordered back, then according to Hampton he "obeyed with wonderful promptness and alacrity."

One of the sad incidents of the war occurred in this last gallant charge of the Eighth Texas Cavalry, numbering as Hampton observed them somewhere from sixty to ninety troopers. Among its recruits was General Hardee's sixteen-year-old son. Hardee, known as "Old Reliable" and beloved by his troops, returned from the attack, filled with enthusiasm over the repulse of Mower, to observe that his only son's horse had come back with an empty saddle.

How many other lads were killed on this field will not likely be known, because Hoke's division of Hardee's corps included an unusual battle group commanded by Brigadier General Laurence Simmons Baker, a native of Gates County, North Carolina, and West Point graduate in 1851. He had served through most of the war in Wade Hampton's cavalry. His last command was called the First Brigade Junior Reserves, and it constituted the largest brigade of Johnston's army. Every soldier in it was *under eighteen years of age.* Nearly every officer was under eighteen. As has been pointed out, these youths were only thirteen when the gun was fired at Fort Sumter. The war was certainly not of their making. Now they were soldiers before they were citizens, volunteers before voters, and veterans before many of them doubtless had ever touched a razor to his face. They have been called "the unripe wheat." The term is apt, for it tells it was not yet their time for the sickle of battle. Bentonville was not their first combat. They had fought with Hoke at Kinston and assisted in the capture of 2,500 Federal prisoners. They had served on the Weldon Railroad in Virginia and had fought at Fort Branch in North Carolina on Christmas Day, 1864, when those of their age should have been sitting around a Christmas tree. Some day their story will be written more fully, but no account of North Carolina in the Civil War would be complete without reference to their part in the desperately fought, three-day battle of Bentonville.

Hardee's charge that pushed back Mower ended the battle. Some North Carolinians who stood on that field that day had witnessed both the beginning and the end of the Civil War. One was Colonel Hector McKethan of the Fifty-first North Carolina Regiment. Second Lieutenant A. A. McKethan, of Company B summed it up: "Many, as was the case of our colonel and a number of others, saw the sun of the South rise in glory at Bethel, and set in its blood-red sheen at Bentonville."

Johnston retreated, and Sherman entered Goldsboro and Raleigh. Johnston's loss was put at 2,606, Sherman's at 1,646. The Federal cavalry commander, Major General George Stoneman, then engaged in a cavalry raid through western North Carolina, showy, but possessing virtually no strategic importance. Much like beating a dead horse, he lashed about and burned public property and supplies. He placed his name on more roadside markers than in history books, for the war was ending when he began and he encountered scarcely token resistance.

Chapter

LAST SHOT AT APPOMATTOX

In its final phase the war that had been a series of great duels between mobile armies traversing wide areas, settled down to the humdrum of the Petersburg trenches — to corn pone and hog fat for quarter rations and rawhide strips for shoes.

Spectacular clashes occurred from time to time — at Reams' Station, where Harry Heth's division, with its North Carolina units, showed its old-time battle fire; at the Crater, where the inept Burnside was baffled in his effort to mine and carry the Confederate works; on Jubal Early's footloose campaign down the Shenandoah Valley and to the very outskirts of Washington.

Lee detached Early in the summer of 1864 to clear the Shenandoah Valley of Federals advancing against Lynchburg and to create a diversion that would force Grant to detach troops and thereby relieve the pressure tightening against Petersburg. Though the bellicose Early failed to behave to expectations in the exercise of independent command and eventually was relieved because of his unfitness and the clamor of public opinion in the South against him, his campaign brought into fuller focus the talents of two of the more capable young generals developed by the war, the North Carolinian Stephen Dodson Ramseur and the Georgian John B. Gordon. Early caused consternation through the North by his sudden descent on Washington. But he possessed neither the audacity nor perhaps the time to enter the city, defended mainly by departmental clerks while Grant was rushing up reinforcements.

Grant later sent heavy Federal forces against Early under Major General Philip H. Sheridan and created a new "Army of the Shenandoah," which, after an initial defeat at Cedar Creek, severely worsted

Early's army in the second phase of that battle. Ramseur, one of North Carolina's finest contributions to the Confederate high command, was mortally wounded, taken prisoner, and carried to the headquarters of his adversary Sheridan, where he received every attention from his former fellow cadets at West Point who were officers in the Northern army. When he had been appointed major general at twenty-seven, he was the youngest West Point graduate in the Confederate army to attain that rank. Only the night before his death he had received word of the birth of his daughter to his wife of a little less than a year, Ellen Richmond of Milton, North Carolina. His letters to her from Lee's army are a treasured, idyllic bit of North Carolina history and romance.

At last Lee's army was outflanked when Pickett lost the battle of Five Forks. Lee gave the signal for the evacuation of Richmond and began the march toward Appomattox, where on Sunday, April 9, 1865, he surrendered his army on the generous conditions that had been discussed by Lincoln with his generals, and which Grant adopted in his terms of capitulation. The essence of the short convention was

Stephen Dodson Ramseur, left, with fellow West Point Cadet Frank Hooper

that the officers and men agreed not to take up arms again against the United States government.

At Appomattox on the day of the surrender, the Thirtieth North Carolina, commanded by Captain David C. Allen, added the final phrase to the North Carolina motto: "last at Appomattox." The Thirtieth was in the brigade commanded by Brigadier General William Ruffin Cox, of Scotland Neck, which had been led earlier in the war by the intrepid Ramseur. The division was that of Major General Bryan Grimes, who, like Longstreet and some others, was impatient with the idea of surrender, and ordered his men to attack on the very morning when the capitulation was being arranged. Grimes' division had been the one led in many battles by the lamented Robert Emmett Rodes, who fell at Winchester.

Earlier in the day Lee had watched Cox's brigade march past him "with steady step and unbroken line" and, when he had identified it, had exclaimed impetuously, "God bless old North Carolina."

Volumes of approbatory literature could not bestow on the State the honor of such heartfelt praise.

Thus the brigade that had held along the "Bloody Lane" at Antietam, had marched with Stonewall Jackson against Hooker's right flank at Chancellorsville, had cleared the stone walls at Gettysburg and passed through carnivals of bloodletting in the Wilderness, at Spotsylvania and at Cold Harbor, fired the final rounds on the last melancholy morning at Appomattox. Captain Allen credited Company D of the Thirtieth, a company raised in Wake and Granville counties, with the last shots, and insisted on having the regiment and company pinpointed when speakers, including Governor Vance, began to refer to the last shots as coming merely from Grimes' division or from Cox's brigade. Vance had a famous lecture in those postwar days which he called "All About It," and Allen had to correct him when he delivered it before the State legislature. Allen was seated at the time between Generals Grimes and Cox, and since those generals asked him to decide the question of what unit had the honor of firing the last shot, his decision can be regarded as final and official.

Cox sent the Thirtieth to support a battery, then took the balance of the regiment to another part of the field. The Northern line advanced in Captain Allen's front, and he gave it a round of infantry fire, which caused it to hit the ground. Another line advanced on his left, and he changed front and gave it a round also. He was surprised that neither line answered his fire. The Federals merely sought cover and waited. Soon he was ordered to rejoin his brigade. There he learned of the surrender. Apparently the heavy Federal lines already were aware of it, for Allen conceded that otherwise "they would have wiped us from the earth." Such was the story of the last firing before the men went home to their spring plowing.

Joseph E. Johnston's surrender to Sherman was signed in the Bennett farmhouse, near Durham, North Carolina, on April 26, 1865.

The story told about this meeting at the Bennett farmhouse is undoubtedly apocryphal, but it serves to show the abiding friendships existing between many of the officers of the two armies. Sherman had known Johnston in the old army, and many of the hostile officers and staffs had been companions as cadets at West Point. While they waited for the convention of surrender to be drafted, the party talked around a table. Like a group of lawyers fraternizing and discussing telling points after the jury verdict in a spectacular trial, the generals who had been parted for four years in bitter war against each other conversed about the battles and campaigns. Someone brought in a gallon of white corn liquor that had been distilled beyond Governor

Vance's watchful eyes, and the nostalgic conversation, waxing more enthusiastic, dwelt lengthily on companionable days at the Point and in the old army. Finally the papers were brought in and the glasses were pushed back, but John C. Breckinridge, a Kentuckian who could hold his bourbon, turned to Sherman and said, "Come on, 'Cump,' have just one more drink."

"Oh, No!" said Sherman. "If I have another drink, I will be surrendering to Johnston."

So if the South lost the Civil War by a single brigade or ten minutes of time at Gettysburg, it might be appended that it lost by no more than a single drink at the Bennett farmhouse!

The final clash of the war in North Carolina was near Waynesville on May 9. Editor George W. McCoy of Asheville, who studied the war in western North Carolina, stated that the last gun of the war fired at Waynesville on May 10, 1865, was possibly the last gun fired in combat east of the Mississippi.

The Confederate force involved in this futile closing fight was the Sixty-ninth North Carolina Regiment commanded by Colonel James R. Love. The principal element of this unit was the picturesque "Thomas' Legion" of Cherokees led by Colonel William Holland Thomas, an adoptive Cherokee chief. The battle — little more than a skirmish — was fought with a detachment of the Federal General George Stoneman's cavalry command. This Federal regiment, recruited in the North Carolina mountains, bore the designation of the Second North Carolina Cavalry of the Union Army. The regiment was commanded by Lieutenant Colonel William C. Bartlett, who was all but surrounded in Waynesville when Thomas rode into town with an escort of his largest and most formidable appearing Cherokees wearing war paint and feathers and emitting outlandish war whoops.

The skirmish was fought near White Sulphur Springs. The single Federal soldier killed among the casualties was undoubtedly the last battle death in the State. During the truce, while Thomas was demanding Bartlett's surrender in Waynesville, news came that Lee had surrendered to Grant in Virginia, and both sides agreed that it made sense to stop the fighting in the remote North Carolina hills. Red and white Confederates were paroled and went back to their homes, after this clash which "pitted Southern highlander against Southern highlander."

Chapter XV

THE TREASURED PAGE OF THE STORY

SUCH IS AN OUTLINE of the story of North Carolina in the Civil War. Much of the seamy side, much of the glorious have not been touched in so brief an account.

To justify this terrible bloodbath, the loss of the fairest young lives of North and South would be wholly impossible. War and its aftermath are destructive, rending, tearing experiences that usually carry their mark on people for generations. Such has been the American Civil War.

But, more than anything else, the Civil War was a demonstration of impatience, and most often war is simply that. Few could foresee, of course, what a fearful trial it would become, else efforts at conciliation would have been more determined; but all should have known from the pages of history that war is never controllable — that once embarked on, it defies its makers and runs its own whimsical course. Among all the dozens of titles given to this combat between North and South, the most inappropriate is that it was an "Irrepressible Conflict," the term employed by William E. Seward, Lincoln's Secretary of State. Very likely with patience and statesmanship the end of slavery, toward which the best thought of both sections aspired, could have been accomplished in the same period of time at a fraction of the expense and no toll of young lives and maimed bodies. Certainly of all methods of solving controversies war has proved itself the least attractive. And of all wars, this was at once the most sanguinary and unnecessary.

Yet along with the grim and destructive there are ennobling aspects of warfare, as there are of any other phase of life, and in it inspiring men appear whose deeds enrich the pages of history. These are the historical treasures that should be preserved. As has been mentioned earlier in this account, war, unsolicited, broke on North Carolina swiftly, almost unexpectedly. Though long discussed, it came with electrifying suddenness. The brightest page in all the long North Carolina story is the manner in which the State unhesitatingly responded to what the government and the undoubted majority of the people regarded their duty.

Most of the North Carolina soldiers had the fortunate experience of serving under one of the most benign of military leaders, Lee, who had no "Marching Through Georgia," or "A crow couldn't fly over the Shenandoah Valley without carrying its own rations" in his record. He waged warfare of the old style, against hostile armies and not civilian populations. Not for a long time, if ever, will this ideal be restored to combat. Here was a general eminently entitled to carry the Bible with him on his campaigns. He expressed his doctrine to a subordinate general: "I cannot hope that heaven will prosper our cause when we are violating its laws. I shall, therefore, carry on war . . . without offending the sanction of a high civilization and of Christianity." With such an attitude at its head, no wonder the Southern army fought with a fervor that has never been surpassed.

As the North Carolina soldiers straggled home hungry and on foot from Appomattox and the Bennett farmhouse, they could have reflected that no defeated army ever was entitled to greater pride in its achievements. Perhaps the finest sentiments at this dark hour came from the State's noted soldier, Robert F. Hoke, who in his farewell address to his division, on May 1, 1865, spoke the ringing words that might uplift North Carolinians for generations:

"You are paroled prisoners, not slaves. The love of liberty which led you into the contest burns as brightly in your hearts as ever. Cherish it. Associate it with the history of your past. Transmit it to your children. Teach them the rights of freemen and teach them to maintain them. Teach them the proudest day in all your proud career was that on which you enlisted as Southern soldiers."

To this may be added the sentiment of the great Zeb Vance, who in a partial paragraph summed up the story of the exalting struggle for Southern independence:

". . . a simple agricultural people, unused to war, without manufactures, without ships, shut out from the world and supposed to be effeminated and degenerated by African slavery, yet waged a four years' contest against four times their numbers, and ten times their means, supplementing all their necessities, and improvising all their material almost out of dreary wastes of chaos; how that their generals wrought out campaigns not discreditable to the genius of Hannibal, Caius Julius, Marlborough and Napoleon; whilst their gently nurtured soldiers fought and marched and endured with the courage of the Grecian phalanx, the steadiness of the Roman Legion, and the endurance of the British Lion — and all because the Southern people had preserved their lofty souls and gallant spirits of their ancestry; had treasured up the traditions of chivalry and personal honor which their fathers had bequeathed them as the highest glory of a race . . . the great lesson which this age is striving to forget, that States will be as their men are, that men will be as their souls are, sordid or lofty as they are taught."

ACKNOWLEDGMENTS

The need for a clear and concise narrative of North Carolina's part in the Civil War has long been apparent. This need has at last been fulfilled through the generosity of Mr. Glenn Tucker, whose outstanding reputation as historian and author is well known throughout the United States. Mr. Tucker is a former Indiana newspaperman who now makes his home in Flat Rock, North Carolina. He was previously a member of The North Carolina Confederate Centennial Commission and is author of such works as *High Tide at Gettysburg, Poltroons and Patriots, Tecumseh: Vision of Glory, Hancock the Superb,* and *Chickamauga,* all published by Bobbs-Merrill.

Of the many persons who contributed to the publication of *Front Rank,* special thanks must be paid to Dr. Christopher Crittenden, Director of the State Department of Archives and History; Mrs. Memory F. Blackwelder and Mrs. Elizabeth Wilborn of the Department's Division of Publications; and to Mr. John R. Peacock of High Point, North Carolina, for their editorial assistance.

We express our appreciation also to Mr. Kenneth Whitsett for the cover illustration and to Mr. Bill Ballard whose drawings so well illustrate Mr. Tucker's narrative.

The majority of the photographs used in *Front Rank* were reproduced by Mrs. Madlin Futrell of the Department of Archives and History. For the copy of the Cameron telegram on page 8, we are indebted to Mr. Jim Tolbert of the North Carolina Collection, University of North Carolina Library.

Finally, this publication could not have been made possible without the able work of the Commission's editorial staff and the assistance of Mr. William Loftin and Mr. David Ramsey of Heritage Printers, Charlotte.

Colonel Hugh Dortch, *Chairman*
The North Carolina Confederate
Centennial Commission

LEE COUNTY LIBRARY SYSTEM
3 3262 00150 1656